HOW TO GUIDE
GIRL SCOUT DAISIES THROUGH

5 FLOWERS,
4 STORIES,
3 CHEERS FOR ANIMALS!

It's Your Story–
TELL IT!

A Leadership
Journey

Girl Scouts of the USA

girl scouts

CHAIR,
NATIONAL BOARD
OF DIRECTORS
Connie L. Lindsey

CHIEF
EXECUTIVE
OFFICER
Kathy Cloninger

CHIEF OPERATING
OFFICER
Jan Verhage

VICE PRESIDENT,
PROGRAM
Eileen Doyle

WRITTEN BY Valerie Takahama, Andrea Bastiani Archibald,
Jackie Glassman and Laura J. Tuchman
ILLUSTRATED BY Susan Swan
DESIGNED BY Rocco Alberico
EXECUTIVE EDITOR: Laura J. Tuchman
ART & PRODUCTION: Douglas Bantz, Ellen Kelliher,
Sarah Micklem, Sheryl O'Connell, Lesley Williams
DIRECTOR, PROGRAM RESOURCES: Suzanne Harper

© 2010 by Girl Scouts of the USA

First published in 2010 by Girl Scouts of the USA
420 Fifth Avenue, New York, NY 10018-2798
www.girlscouts.org

ISBN: 978-0-88441-755-2

Printed in Italy

1 2 3 4 5 6 7 8 9/17 16 15 14 13 12 11 10

CREDITS: Page 33, Valerie Takahama; Pages 41 & 101 Kimberley Stoney;
Pages 32, 54 & 55, Monika Melnychuk

This publication was made
possible by a generous grant
from the Dove Self-Esteem Fund.

Mixed Sources
Product group from well-managed
forests and other controlled sources
www.fsc.org   Cert no. SQS-COC-100209
© 1996 Forest Stewardship Council

Text printed on Fedrigoni Cento 40 percent de-inked, post-
consumer fibers and 60 percent secondary recycled fibers.
Covers printed on Prisma artboard FSC Certified mixed
sources.

CONTENTS

Building girls' **confidence**

is the goal of this *It's Your Story—Tell It!* journey.

Building confidence every day.

Girl Scouting builds girls of **courage, confidence, and character,** who make the world a better place.

That's our **mission.** And we do it through 3 keys to leadership: **Discover + Connect +Take Action**

On this journey...

Girl Scout Daisies learn to care for animals and for themselves.

Then they get creative—through murals, dance, drawing, puppets—and tell their story of caring for animals.

Caring for animals, caring for themselves— that builds confidence!

Imagine how far a Daisy can go and how much she can do—for herself *and* the world—when she has confidence.

Now, multiply that confidence by 550,000, the number of Girl Scout Daisies in the world. These Daisies will be leaders in their own lives and leaders in the world—because they Discover, Connect, and Take Action. That's a future to journey toward!

What to pack for the journey!

Girl Scout leadership journeys invite girls to explore a theme through many experiences and from many perspective— through the 3 keys to leadership: **Discover + Connect + Take Action**

All the joys of travel are built right in! So fill your suitcase with everything you need for an amazing trip that will change girls' lives!

It's Your PLANET Love It!

It's Your WORLD Change It!

It's your STORY Tell It!

Discover

Connect

Take Action

Destination: Leadership!

The Girls' Book

Fun activities and recipes, engaging stories and creative projects let girls . . . meet new people, explore new things, make memories, gather keepsakes, and earn badges—all while exploring a theme through the 3 keys to leadership!!

The Adult Guide

Fun activities to get girls thinking and doing while strengthening their team-building, creativity, and sense of self—as they explore the 3 keys to leadership! Plus: healthful snacks, and tips for Story Times and other "chats" with girls.

Your Wider Community

Reach out to local experts on . . . storytelling, animal care, the arts. And to local partners: zoos, animal shelters and agencies, libraries, and arts groups.

Your Enthusiasm

And your creativity, your partnership with girls and families, and, most important, your willingness to learn by doing, right alongside the girls!

Stories+ Creativity =2 Fun Ways to Build Girls' Confidence as Leaders

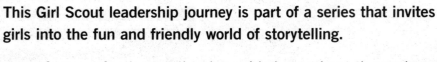

This Girl Scout leadership journey is part of a series that invites girls into the fun and friendly world of storytelling.

Stories are fundamental to how girls learn about themselves and the world.

Stories allow girls to experience the variety of the world all around them, and that develops their empathy, tolerance, and acceptance of others.

Stories sharpen girls' minds and spark their imaginations.

Stories inspire and motivate.

Stories teach girls how to lead in their own lives and in the world.

Story Time! Throughout this journey, the Daisies hear the flower friends' stories and tell their own stories. A Story Time is built into each sample session, so invite a range of guests to serve as readers—older girls, family members, and professionals in the community.

Daisy-age children

love hearing stories in full, so consider reading the girls all the stories aloud at one time, even in the first session or a special kick-off event! Then at each subsequent session, go back and enjoy the story with the girls section by section, as each sample session plan indicates.

Try telling stories

with hand gestures, different voices for different characters, and pauses to give the girls a chance to react to what's happening. Daisies will enjoy seeing you "perform"—and they'll learn fun storytelling techniques to use when they tell their own stories on this journey and throughout their lives!

A book for every girl!

So that girls can enjoy the journey stories (both words and pictures) whenever they like, it's important that each girl has her own journey book. They can draw inspiration from the book and gain confidence in telling their own stories all along the way. This journey book may be the first of many mementos the girls will cherish throughout their years in Girl Scouting and beyond!

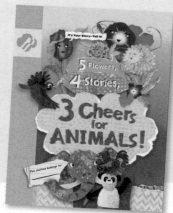

Creativity Counts!

Creative expression is one of the best ways to strengthen young girls' self-esteem. So along this journey, the **Daisies create and add to three big animal-themed projects built right into the Sample Sessions**.

1. Team Animal Mural
This team effort can also serve as a colorful backdrop for each Daisy gathering. The girls might share the mural at the journey's final celebration or present it to incoming Daisies as an invitation to this animal-filled journey.

2. Team Birdbath
This team effort stores all the animal-care ideas the girls learn along the journey.

3. All About Me Nests
These give each girl a place to keep items that show how she cares for herself on this journey and in life.

These projects let the Daisies:

- express themselves and experiment
- lift up one another through encouragement and teamwork
- have fun and let their creativity flow!

Don't Judge, Just Enjoy! Like all activities on this journey, these projects are not to be judged for "ability"; let the girls be creative!

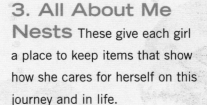

Fun extras for the journey!

Animal sculptures from found objects
For inspiration, check out the sculptures by Deborah Butterfield, on page 38 of the girls' book! The Daisies might use twigs, stones, shells, bottle caps, paper packaging, or anything they can find!

Thank-you cards for guest speakers—ones that explain what the Daisies learned that led to their earning a journey award.

You helped us earn our Red Robin Award!

Animal guessing game
Place animal pictures in a box, ask each girl to choose one (without showing it to anyone), and then take turns giving clues about the care the animal needs as the other girls guess the animal!

Family Kickoff Event
Consider starting this journey with a family event where everyone joins in to make the Team Birdbath (from papier mâché or found objects). See pages 32–33.

Why Self-Esteem Matters!

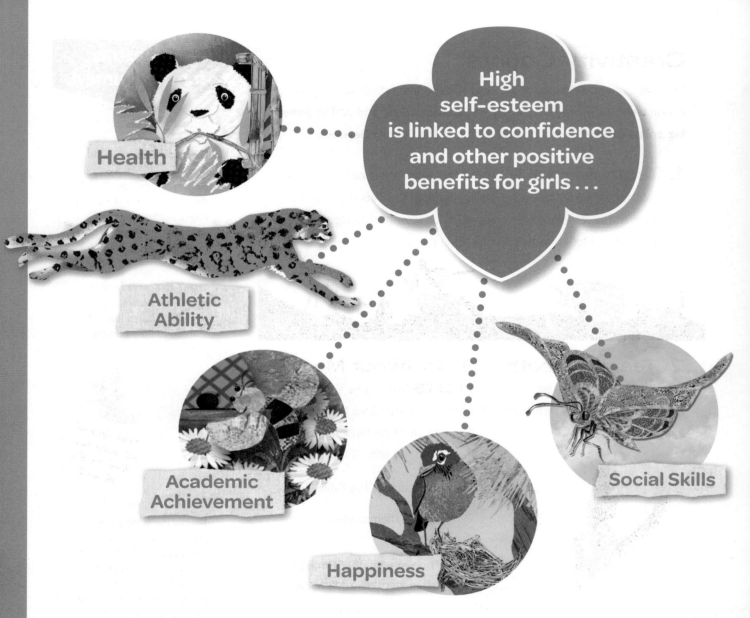

Health

High self-esteem is linked to confidence and other positive benefits for girls . . .

Athletic Ability

Academic Achievement

Happiness

Social Skills

Self-esteem means how a girl feels about herself—her abilities, her body, her capacity to seek and meet challenges in the world. On average, the self-esteem of Daisy-age girls is relatively high. Keeping the Daisies' self-esteem high is one of the goals of this journey. That way, as the girls grow, they're more likely to avoid the drop in self-esteem that is so typical in adolescence. Without that drop, their confidence can soar!

Session Plans Make the Most of Daisies' Skills

The Sample Session plans starting on page 28 offer opportunities for the girls to enhance their skills and develop new ones while taking into account the abilities and needs of Daisy-age girls. When planning additional creative adventures, keep in mind that kindergartners and first-graders:

have loads of energy and need to run, walk, and play outside.	*So they will enjoy going on nature walks and outdoor scavenger hunts.*
are great builders and budding artists, though still developing their fine-motor skills.	*So encourage them to express themselves and their creativity by making things with their hands. Girls may need assistance, however, holding scissors, cutting in a straight line, etc.*
love to move and dance.	*So they might especially enjoy marching like a penguin, dancing like a dolphin, or acting out how they might care for animals in the jungle!*
are concrete thinkers and focused on the "here and now."	*So show them firsthand how animals are cared for—at shelters, farms, or zoos, and by practicing ways they can care for animals.*
are just learning about number concepts, time, and money.	*So take opportunities to count out supplies together, or even the legs on a caterpillar!*
don't always have the words for what they want to say.	*So having them draw a picture of something they are trying to communicate is frequently easier for them and more meaningful.*
know how to follow simple directions and respond well to recognition for doing so.	*So be specific and offer only one direction at a time. Acknowledging when the girls have followed directions well will also increase their motivation for listening and following again.*

Promoting Well-Being Along the Journey

Girl Scouting is guided by a positive philosophy of inclusion that benefits all. On this journey, especially, it is hoped that girls will increase their feelings of being powerful, capable, and strong as they enhance their skills and develop new ones. So, as the Girl Scout Law says, "be a sister to every Girl Scout." Ask whether any girls are new to town, have a disability, don't speak English as a first language, or have parents getting a divorce. Often what counts most is being open-minded and aware, staying flexible, and creatively varying your approach with the girls.

Birdbath Award

What it means for Daisies: They can say: "Animals need care; I need care. I can do both."

How Daisies earn it: They name one way they can care for animals and one way they can care for themselves (Sessions 1-3).

When Daisies receive it: Session 4

WHERE TO PUT THE GARDEN PATCH?

The three awards that girls earn on this journey fit on a colorful garden patch background that can be placed on the Daisies' tunics—wherever they like!

Consider presenting the background patch to the girls at their first gathering to spark their excitement for the journey and its awards.

IF A GIRL MISSES AN AWARD STEP . . .

Find a way for her to do something similar to what she missed so she can still earn the award with her group. Your goal is to guide her to have the same learning and growing opportunity—and to understand how she can contribute to the team.

Red Robin Award

What it means for Daisies: They can use their new knowledge and creativity to teach others how to care for animals.

How Daisies earn it: They choose animal care tips to share with others and then tell this "story of animal care" in a creative way with a Red Robin Project (Sessions 4-8).

When Daisies receive it: Session 9

Tula Award

What it means for Daisies: They have gained courage and confidence in teaching others about animal care.

How Daisies earn it: They share with one another the good feelings they experienced as they taught others in their community about animal care.

When Daisies receive it: Final Celebration

LADDER OF LEADERSHIP

As Girl Scouts take journeys and earn the awards, they're climbing a ladder that lets them be leaders in their own lives and in the world! Pass it on!

It's Your World—Change It!

It's Your Story—Tell It!

It's Your Planet—Love It!

Ambassadors raise their voices to advocate for issues they care about.

Girls move dreams forward!

Ambassadors learn that leaders aim for justice.

AMBASSADOR

Seniors learn that leaders have a vision and can move the world a step closer to it.

Girls see how much sisterhood does for the world!

Seniors find out what leaders can sow for Earth.

SENIOR

Cadettes develop the people skills that leaders need.

Girls put the ME in media.

Cadettes become leaders in clearing the air!

CADETTE

Juniors learn that leaders need power—their own, their team's, and their community's.

Girls explore all the roles open to them in life.

Juniors bring energy solutions to the world.

JUNIOR

Brownies go on a quest to find the three keys to leadership.

Girls explore their place in the wide world of girls.

Brownies take the lead in saving Earth's water.

BROWNIE

Girls learn they can care for animals and themselves.

Daisies have fun—and learn leadership skills—in the garden.

Daisies learn to protect Earth's treasures.

DAISY

13

What You'll Find in Each Sample Session Plan

THE JOURNEY SNAPSHOT gives an overview of what's ahead

Journey activities are sequenced to give girls lots of fun and exciting challenges centered around earning the journey's three leadership awards. But don't feel you and the girls must do everything in the Sample Sessions or in the order given. Think of journey activities as pieces that can be mixed, matched, and coordinated according to the needs of your group of Daisies.

THE SAMPLE SESSION PLANS
JOURNEY SNAPSHOT

SESSION 1 Starting Our Animal Adventure	The Daisies begin to identify ways they can care for animals. They start a Team Animal Mural and create a Team Birdbath.
SESSION 2 Caring That Counts	The Daisies explore the many ways that caring for animals is like caring for themselves. They create All About Me Nests.
SESSION 3 Tail Tales	The Daisies use their imaginations and problem-solving skills as they continue to explore how the needs of animals are similar to their own.
SESSION 4 All Creatures Great and Special	The Daisies begin to explore how animals, like people, are unique, including in the ways they communicate and move. The girls earn their Birdbath Award.
SESSION 5 Out and About with Animals	The Daisies learn more about needs of animals in preparation for teaching others about animal care.
SESSION 6 A Postcard Is Worth a Thousand Words	The Daisies continue to explore the needs of animals and use critical-thinking skills to begin to focus on specific animal needs in their community.
SESSION 7 Inspired by Animals	The Daisies continue to explore how caring for animals resembles caring for themselves. They begin their Red Robin Project to educate others about animal care.
SESSION 8 What Animals Tell Us	The Daisies strengthen their communication skills as they progress on their Red Robin Project.
SESSION 9 Teaching Others with Confidence!	The Daisies educate and inspire others on animal care with their Red Robin Project, building their own confidence along the way. They earn their Red Robin Award.
SESSION 10 Many Skills to Learn	The Daisies begin to understand how caring for animals, and caring for themselves, makes them feel.
THE FINAL CELEBRATION Celebrate Our Learning!	The Daisies celebrate what they've learned and their growing confidence in caring for animals and themselves. They earn their Tula Award.

AT A GLANCE gives the session's goal, activities, and recommended materials.

TOWARD THE AWARD ICONS indicate activities that step girls toward a leadership award.

CEREMONIES, opening and closing, mark the Daisies' time together as special.

SAMPLE SESSION 1
Starting Our Animal Adventure

COME JOIN IN THE FUN!

Consider turning this first Daisy gathering into a family kickoff event where everyone joins in to make the Team Birdbath. (The Birdbath will hold the animal care ideas the girls learn along the journey; it symbolizes their new knowledge, their ability to care for animals, and their growing confidence as leaders.) Make use of the letter to the Friends and Family Network on page OO to publicize the kickoff!

FIRST-YEAR DAISIES? FIRST THINGS FIRST

If any girls in the group are new to Girl Scouting, explain that a Daisy Circle is something they form to mark special times, such as:

- the start of a Girl Scout Daisy gathering
- welcoming new girls and visitors
- sharing ideas
- making group decisions
- listening to the Daisy Flower Garden stories
- any time they want to talk as a group

AT A GLANCE

Goal: Daisies identify ways they can care for animals.

- Opening Ceremony: Animals Around the World (Bald Eagle: United States)
- Team Animal Mural
- Story Time: "Welcome to this Amazing Animal Adventure"
- Snack Time: Ants on a Log
- Toward the Award: Building a Team Birdbath
- Closing Ceremony: Keeping the Girl Scout Promise

MATERIALS

- **Arrival Activity:** copies of the girls' book, one for each girl
- **Opening Ceremony: Animals Around the World (Bald Eagle: United States):** picture of a bald eagle (page OO); garden patches for the Daisy leadership awards (one for each girl)
- **Team Animal Mural:** mural-size paper; markers, crayons, glue, and assorted craft material; a large sheet of paper and marker for jotting down the girls' ideas
- **Snack Time:** see Ants on a Log (see recipe, page OO in the girls' book
- **Building a Team Birdbath:** papier mâché materials (see recipe, page OO); shallow bowl or found/recycled materials, such as a pie tin and can or a clay pot saucer and a pot; colored tissue paper and other decorative materials; paper and markers or crayons
- **Closing Ceremony: Keeping the Girl Scout Promise:** Girl Scout Promise written on a large sheet of paper

PREPARE AHEAD

- Chat with any assistants about what they will do before and during the session. Lay out or hang the paper for the Team Animal Mural. **Prepare materials** for making the Team Birdbath. If using papier mâché, cover the work space with newspaper or plastic, and place bowls for starch and paper on top. **Write the Girl Scout Promise** on a large sheet of paper for the Closing Ceremony.

AS GIRLS ARRIVE

Greet the girls and invite them to explore their book, especially page TK with its many hidden pictures of animals in the Daisy Flower Garden.

Opening Ceremony: Animals Around the World (Bald Eagle: United States)

Gather the girls in a circle and ask them to take turns introducing themselves and naming one thing they like about animals. Start them off by saying something like: *My name is Ana. I like that my dog loves fetching a ball.*

Then let the girls know that they are about to begin an exciting Girl Scout journey about caring for animals. Say something like:

- *A journey is an adventure where you see new places, meet new people, and have lots of fun.*
- *Our journey, led by beautiful flower friends, begins in the United States.*

Show the girls the picture of a bald eagle at right, and explain that the eagle is the national bird of the United States of America. Depending where you and the Daisies are, you might explain that the United States is the country where they live, or where they may have lived at some point in their lives.

Then ask if anyone knows the meaning of the word "national." If they don't, offer a simple explanation. If you live in the United States, you might say:

"National" means belonging to a country. The bald eagle is our national bird, just as the Stars and Stripes is our national flag.

Then share this fun fact about the bald eagle: *Bald eagles build the largest nests of any bird in North America.*

INTRODUCE THE JOURNEY'S AWARDS

After sharing the fun fact about the bald eagle with the girls, you might give each Daisy her garden patch for the journey's awards. Let the girls know that on this journey, they will have a chance to earn three awards that show their special place as leaders in Girl Scouts. Explain that each award will be placed on the garden patch, which they can wear on their Daisy tunic.

28

29

14

STORY TIME, for fun and learning, ties the girls' book and the Daisies' group time together!

ACTIVE TIME activities get girls moving!

WHAT TO SAY A full script for you to use! Must you follow it? No! Let it guide you but be yourself!

CREATIVE ACTIVITIES encourage creativity, self-expression and teamwork.

SNACKS offer girls healthful, animal-themed energy boosters.

Story Time: "The First Stories"

Today the girls will enjoy "The First Stories" chapter their book, in which each flower friend makes up a story about how she got her color and how she's special. After reading as much of the story as you have time for today, encourage girls to discuss what makes them special. Use prompts like these to get them talking:

- *In the story today, the flower friends notice what makes them special. What's special and unique about you? Do you speak another language? Do you know magic tricks?*
- *Red Robin shares how she became red. Think about what you just shared about yourself, and describe how you became that way. If you speak another language, for example, how did you learn it?*

team talk!

Spin-a-Tale

Invite the girls to sit in a circle. Ask who can retell the story of how Robin, the Red Robin, became red from today's story. Once the story has been told, explain that Robin's story is a special kind of folktale that tells why certain things in nature came to be. These folktales answer the question, "Why?" but are not true stories.

You might say: "Pourquoi" is the French word for "why," and pourquoi *tales are old legends that explain why certain things happened, usually things having to do with animals and the natural world.*

Give some examples of some famous pourquoi tales, such as *How the Leopard Lost Its Spots* and *Why Mosquitoes Buzz in People's Ears.* Now start a story about how an animal got to be the way it is (such as how the zebra got its stripes) and invite the girls to continue the story, with each girl adding a new part, until they've gone all the way around the circle and made up their own pourquoi tale. If you are able, record the story as the girls make it up. When it is finished, make copies on DVD or in an audio file for each girl to bring or send home.

ALL FOR ONE AND ONE FOR ALL
Cooperative learning—one of the three Girl Scout processes—happens when all members of a group team up toward a common goal. Structured team activities, such as "Spin-a-Tale," encourage the girls to think and create together. Each person's part is important and key to the finished product.

Snack Time! Incredible, Edible Nests
Gather the girls around the table with your sample nest and recipe ingredients. Then invite each girl to assemble her own—and enjoy!

Fly, Fly Away

In "The First Stories," Red Robin shares that soon it will be time for her to fly to Mexico for the winter. Invite the girls to spread their wings and "fly" like Red Robin. (This can be done indoors or out.)

- Have each girl choose three streamers for each "wing."
- Then show them how to clasp the streamers together in each hand. Have them practice moving their arms up and down.
- Next, show them how to make circles or other shapes with their wings.
- When they're ready, turn on the music and invite the girls to "fly, fly away!" by dancing, skipping, running, etc., to the rhythm as they hold their crepe paper wings at shoulder height, and let them move through the air.
- Change the music every minute or so to encourage the girls to move in time to the new beat. Invite another girl to lead the flock each time the music changes.
- For an added challenge, call out the names of birds and suggest that the girls move like each bird. (Examples: waddle like a penguin, hover like a hummingbird, run like a roadrunner, stand like...

Moving to music may give the girls ... ... their Red Robin Award ... ... along this journey. They might even want to present to their audience in a way that uses movement and music!

MAKE MEANING OF MUSIC
Since creativity is a theme of this journey—and that includes the music—take this opportunity to share with the girls the names of the songs and composers you used for the "Fly, Fly Away" activity. Have them share which music they liked best, and why. Also ask which they didn't like, and why.

GET CREATIVE!

Team Animal Mural

Show the Daisies the large sheet of paper, or other art materials you've chosen, and explain that as they learn about animals on this journey, they'll team up to place each animal on their Team Animal Mural.

- Explain to the girls: *A mural is a big picture that tells a story. Usually a mural is so big, it covers a whole wall! Our mural will tell the story of all the animals we meet on this journey.*
- Guide the girls to write "Our Animal Mural" (or another title of their choice) across the top of the mural in large letters. Then invite each girl to use the art materials on hand to make one part of a bald eagle. You might say: *Let's each pick one part of the eagle to make, and then we'll put all our parts together to make one eagle! Here's what we'll need: two wings, two legs and feet, a head, body, and tail.*
- If there are more Daisies than eagle parts, suggest that the girls pair up to make a part together. Or perhaps the girls would like to make two eagles for the mural. They might even be placed at the top, one on each side of the mural's title.

As girls make their eagle parts, remind them that eagles build the largest nests in North America. Then say something like: *On this journey, you will each build a small nest during our next Daisy time together. We're going to call these nests our All About Me Nests, because they will hold all the things you know and learn about caring for yourself.* Then ask:

What do you have in your lives now that is like a nest?

- *What is in your "nest"?*

Ask the girls if they have any ideas for how they would like to make and decorate their All About Me Nests, and jot their ideas on a large sheet of paper. If they don't have any ideas, suggest that they might use shoe boxes or another type of container.

TEAMING UP FOR ART AND CONFIDENCE!
Each time the girls team up for their mural or another art project, they are taking part in cooperative learning—working together toward a common goal. That means they're gaining social skills, too, such as taking turns and listening to others. And that builds confidence!

Story Time: "Welcome to This Amazing Animal Adventure"

Introduce the journey's Flower Garden story by reading the short introduction on page 5 of the girls' book. When you finish, spark the girls' thinking by asking a few questions, like these:

- *What animals have you seen near where you live?*
- *Have you ever cared for animals in your yard or neighborhood? For example, have you ever put out a bird feeder or a birdbath?*
- *Have you ever cared for a pet, either your own or a friend's or neighbor's? What did you do? What did you like most about taking care of the pet?*
- *What is the most unusual animal you've ever seen? Where did you see it? What did it look like? Who takes care of it and how?*

After the Daisies have a chance to answer, say something like:

On this journey, you'll meet lots of animals. You'll hear how they are cared for, and how they stay safe and protected, and how they talk with one another—and you'll have a chance to care for them, too!

team talk!

Engaging the Daisies in discussions, such as ones about the journey's Flower Garden stories, gives the girls opportunities to sharpen their speaking skills—and gain confidence! The ability to speak well and communicate thoughts clearly is a great leadership skill. So keep the Daisies chattering!

Snack Time! Ants on a Log
This snack is featured on page 75 of the girls' book. For the Daisies to make it together as a group, clean and cut celery stalks into 2- to 3-inch pieces, making enough pieces for each girl. Have cheese (or hummus) and raisins prepared, and spoons handy to use as spreaders, so girls can decorate their logs.

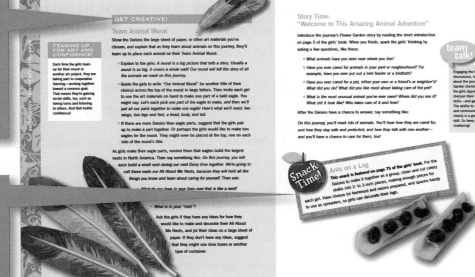

Creating a Network of Journey Resources

GO ONLINE FOR LETTERS HOME

Visit the Journeys section of girlscouts.org for letters and forms to start your Friends and Family Network and keep its members informed and motivated to join in the fun! You'll find:

- Welcome Letter

- Checklist for Friends and Family Network

- Take-Home letters for help with journey snacks and art supplies

You'll get a break and expand the girls' awareness of community by asking family members, friends, and friends of friends to visit and enhance the Daisies' gatherings. So go ahead and "hand off" activities and prep steps to a Daisy Friends and Family Network. Here are some tips:

- Before the journey begins, aim for a brief get-together (even online!) with parents, caregivers, relatives, and friends.

- Find out who likes to do what, identify assistants for various activities, and see who has time for behind-the-scenes preparations, gathering supplies (pads, markers, glitter, glue), or snack duty.

- Keep in mind that in some families, an aunt, older sibling, cousin, or other adult may be most able to participate.

More Print and Online Journey Resources

☐ *Girl Scout Safety Activity Checkpoints* detail the safety net provided for girls in Girl Scouting. Seek them out from your council and keep them handy!

☐ **Journey maps, in the Journeys section of girlscouts.org,** show you and the girls how to mix the outdoors, trips, badges, and Girl Scout traditions (including cookies!) into your journey fun.

☐ *It's Your Journey—Customize It!* is your guide to making the most of Girl Scout leadership journeys.

☐ *Volunteer Essentials* is your guide to all things Girl Scouts! Seek it out from your council.

☐ **Online activities** for girls to enjoy on their own, with friends, and with their Daisy group, are at www.girlscouts.org/itsyourstory.

DAISY JOURNEY PEOPLE POWER

FRIENDS & FAMILY NETWORK: Name	Willing to help with:	Phone and e-mail address

COUNCIL CONTACTS: Name	Willing to help with:	Phone and e-mail address

LOCAL EXPERTS: Name	Area of expertise	Phone and e-mail address

Girl Scout Traditions and Ceremonies

Traditions and ceremonies have always been part of the fun of being a Girl Scout. They show girls they are part of a sisterhood: They connect girls to one another, to their sister Girl Scouts and Girl Guides around the world, and to the generations of girls who were Girl Scouts before them.

This journey offers frequent opportunities to gather in Daisy Friendship Circles and other ceremonies. Ceremonies give girls a chance to share their strengths, hopes, and accomplishments, and experience the power of belonging. So involve the Daisies in creating new traditions—even silly songs! Your Girl Scout council may have its own traditions that you can enjoy along the journey, too. Here are a few of the most enduring Girl Scout traditions:

GIRL SCOUT SIGN

The Girl Scout sign is made when saying the Girl Scout Promise. The sign is formed with the right hand, using the thumb to hold down the little finger, leaving the middle fingers extended to represent the Promise's three parts.

QUIET SIGN

The Quiet Sign is a way to silence a crowd without shouting at anyone. The sign is made by holding up the right hand with all five fingers extended. It refers to the original Fifth Law of Girl Scouting: A Girl Scout is courteous.

GIRL SCOUT HANDSHAKE

The Girl Scout handshake is the way many Girl Guides and Girl Scouts greet each other. They shake their left hands while making the Girl Scout sign with their right hand. The left-handed handshake represents friendship because the left hand is closer to the heart than the right.

FRIENDSHIP CIRCLE

This circle is often formed at the end of meetings or campfires as a closing ceremony. Everyone gathers in a circle, and each girl crosses her right arm over her left and holds hands with the person on each side. With everyone silent, the leader starts by squeezing the hand of the person next to her. One by one, each girl passes on the squeeze until it travels around the full circle.

GIRL SCOUTS!

As Girls Scouts celebrates its 100th anniversary in 2012, this leadership journey is a reminder of the long-cherished Girl Scout tradition of girls creating change in their local and global communities. *It's Your Story—Tell It!* continues the story of Girl Scouting—a story of leadership and making the world a better place.

GIRL SCOUT DAYS TO CELEBRATE

- **Founder's Day**
  October 31
  Juliette "Daisy" Gordon Low's birthday

- **World Thinking Day**
  February 22
  A day for Girl Scouts and Girl Guides throughout the world to think about one another

- **Girl Scout Birthday**
  March 12
  The day in 1912 when Juliette Gordon Low officially registered the organization's first 18 girl members in Savannah, Georgia

THE GIRL SCOUT LAW

I will do my best to be

honest and fair,

friendly and helpful,

considerate and caring,

courageous and strong, and

responsible for what I say and do,

and to

respect myself and others,

respect authority,

use resources wisely,

make the world a better place, and

be a sister to every Girl Scout.

THE GIRL SCOUT PROMISE

On my honor, I will try:
To serve God* and my country,
To help people at all times,
And to live by the Girl Scout Law.

*Girl Scouts of the USA makes no attempt to define or interpret the word "God" in the Girl Scout Promise. It looks to individual members to establish for themselves the nature of their spiritual beliefs. When making the Girl Scout Promise, individuals may substitute wording appropriate to their own spiritual beliefs for the word "God."

Keys to Girl Leadership

Girl Scouting prepares girls to be leaders—in their own daily lives and in the world around them. We do this through the Girl Scout Leadership Experience, pictured below, which is the basis for everything girls do in Girl Scouting. The three keys to leadership—Discover (self), Connect (team up and network with others), and Take Action (make a difference in the world)—are a shorthand way of capturing all of the 15 national leadership benefits girls receive in Girl Scouting.

As you can see in the charts on pages 110–111, all of the experiences in this journey have been created to engage girls in exploring these three keys to leadership. In fact, that's what makes a Girl Scout journey so special: Everything girls and their adult guides need to explore the leadership keys is built right in!

So all along the way, you will be guiding the Daisies toward leadership skills and qualities they can use right now—and all their lives. Keep in mind that the intended benefits to girls are the cumulative result of traveling through an entire journey—and everything else girls experience in Girl Scouting!

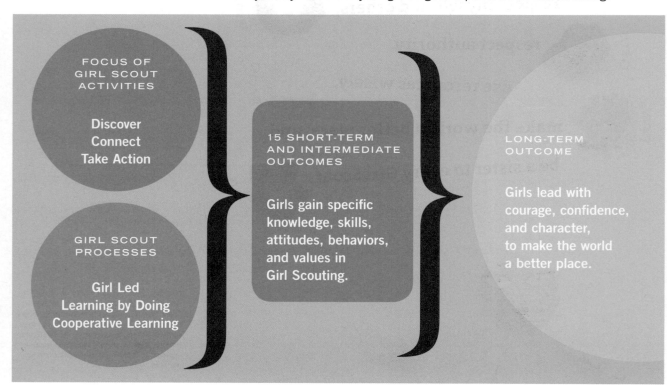

FOCUS OF GIRL SCOUT ACTIVITIES

Discover
Connect
Take Action

GIRL SCOUT PROCESSES

Girl Led
Learning by Doing
Cooperative Learning

15 SHORT-TERM AND INTERMEDIATE OUTCOMES

Girls gain specific knowledge, skills, attitudes, behaviors, and values in Girl Scouting.

LONG-TERM OUTCOME

Girls lead with courage, confidence, and character, to make the world a better place.

How Girls Have Fun in Girl Scouting

In Girl Scouting, girls enjoy activities based on the three keys to leadership and built on three processes that make Girl Scouting unique from school and other extracurricular activities. The keys and processes are built right into the journey for you—in the Sample Session plans! So you know a little more about how the processes play out for Daisies, here's a quick summary:

Girl Led means girls play an active part in figuring out the what, where, when, how, and why of their activities. Encourage them to lead the planning, decision-making, learning, and fun as much as possible. This ensures that girls experience leadership opportunities as they prepare to become active participants in their communities. With Daisies, you could:

- help girls decide the who, what, where, when, and how of activities
- identify activities that girls can take the lead on
- encourage girls to volunteer for projects they think they would be good at

Learning by Doing engages girls in continuous cycles of action and reflection that result in deeper understanding of concepts and mastery of skills. As they participate in meaningful activities and then reflect on them, girls explore their own questions, discover answers, gain new skills, and share ideas and observations. It's important for girls to connect their experiences to their lives and apply what they have learned to future experiences in and outside of Girl Scouting. With Daisies, you could:

- set up opportunities for girls to explore and create
- demonstrate hands-on activities that require assistance from a girl
- develop activities that get girls "out of their seat" and involved

Cooperative Learning has girls work together toward goals with mutual respect and collaboration. Working together in all-girl environments encourages girls to feel powerful and emotionally and physically safe, and allows them to experience a sense of belonging. With Daisies, you could:

- give girls examples of what cooperation and collaboration look like
- create activities for girls that must be completed in groups
- promote social skills, such as listening and taking turns

KEEP IT GIRL LED

Yes, even our youngest members can take the lead! From beginning to end, keep your eye on what the girls want to do and the direction they seem to be taking. It's the approach begun by Juliette Gordon Low: When she and her associates couldn't decide on a new direction, she often said, "Let's ask the girls!"

Girl-led experiences are built right into this journey to make it easy for you.

At each session, ask the girls for their own thoughts on what they've done or discussed.

What It All Means for Girls

All activities in this leadership journey relate to Discovering, Connecting, and Taking Action—the three Girl Scout keys to leadership! Plus, Girl Led, Cooperative Learning, and Learning By Doing processes make the activities fun and powerful for girls. Here, in a role-play activity from Session 3, you can see how these processes and the national Girl Scout outcomes—the benefits we want for girls—play out during a team gathering. The processes and outcomes are so seamless you might not notice them. Throughout the journey, processes and outcomes play out again and again. Before you know it, you'll be using these valuable aspects of Girl Scouting in whatever Daisies do!

This is a good example of the **Cooperative Learning** process, as girls team up to develop and practice decision-making skills.

Role-play activities are also great examples of **Learning by Doing** for girls, as they strengthen and practice their social skills with real-life sample scenarios.

FROM SAMPLE SESSION 3

Role-Play: Choices, Choices

Ask the girls to pair up for some role-play about making decisions. Then read them one of these scenarios (or another that you create based on the girls' discussions, examples from the animal expert who visited, or other situations that have come up along the journey):

Scenario 1

Abby and Ellie are playing catch in Ellie's backyard when they hear a sad little "chirp, chirp" sound coming from the woods. They follow the sound and discover a baby bird on the ground. They look up and see the chick has fallen from a nest in one of the trees.

"Poor little baby bird," cries Abby. "Let's get it back in its nest with its mommy," she suggests.

"Maybe we should go in and tell my mom," says Ellie. "I'm not sure if we should touch it, even though it looks like it wants to get back to its nest right away."

"But the branch is so close, and the baby is so sad," says Abby.

Take on the roles of Ellie and Abby and decide together what you will do: Lift the bird back into its nest or tell Ellie's mom.

Each of these scenarios, in which girls work toward recognizing and considering that other people have thoughts and feelings that are different from their own, is aimed at **Discover Outcome, Girls develop critical thinking skills.**

Scenario 2

Two friends, Pilar and Jessie, are walking to a fair in their town. They are very excited. "I'm going to go on the roller coaster!" Pilar says.

"I can't wait to play the arcade games," says Jessie.

"Yoo hoo!" calls 90-year-old Mrs. Smith from her window, as the girls pass by. Pilar and Jessie stop. Mrs. Smith tells the girls she is not feeling well today and asks, "Will you please walk my dog right now?"

Take on the roles of Pilar and Jessie and decide together what you will do: Walk the dog and be late for the fair, or tell Mrs. Smith that you can't walk her dog.

Though not project-focused, decision-making here is an excellent example of social problem-solving for Daisies, and striving toward the **Take Action Outcome, Girls are resourceful problem-solvers.**

After each pair of girls decides what they will do, have them present their solutions to the full group of Daisies as a short role-play.

After the first scenario, you might point out that there may be other things that the girls might decide to do. For example, the girls can take the dog for a quick walk now, and a longer one after the fair. Ask if they think that might be a good thing to do.

Then wrap up by guiding the Daisies to draw pictures and write captions under them to describe how their decision to help or not help made them feel, and put them in the Team Birdbath. You might use this template:

In this example, girls are learning to compromise by recognizing that what they say and do affects other people. They must consider and balance their and others' needs if everyone is to be satisfied in the end.

Recognizing that what they say and do has an effect on others moves toward the **Discover Outcome, Girls develop positive values**. Girls' recognition that they can act on behalf of themselves and others targets the **Take Action Outcome, Girls advocate for themselves and others.**

Asking girls to identify how they feel after making a decision moves them toward the **Connect Outcome, Girls develop healthy relationships**, as does their decision, if they decided to help, in either scenario.

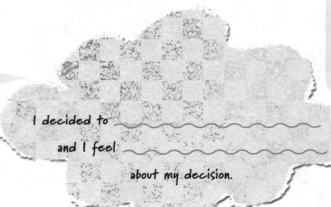

I decided to _____ and I feel _____ about my decision.

Flower Friends, Global Themes

I n *3 Cheers for Animals!,* the flower friends tell stories of visits to their homelands. If the girls already enjoyed *Welcome to the Daisy Flower Garden* or *Between Earth and Sky,* they may remember that the flowers come from various parts of the country and have family all around the world. This makes them a great springboard for exploring various cultures. You might invite teens or adults who grew up in regions other than your own to join a Daisy gathering to talk about their hometowns, and the activities they enjoy there. Guide the Daisies to see that differences are what make people and places—and animals—unique and interesting, and that differences, as well as similarities, are to be respected and appreciated.

Gloria, the morning glory, is purple. She is from Japan and tells the story of her visit home.

Zinni, the zinnia, is spring green. She's from Mexico and tells a story of her visit to a farm there.

Vi, the violet, is from Australia. She's at home in the Daisy garden and enjoys the whole adventure.

Tula, the tulip, is from Holland and her family is originally from Iran. She's a main character all through this journey.

Mari, the marigold, is from Africa and she tells the story of a visit home to the country of Tanzania.

Your Perspective on Leadership

The Girl Scout Leadership Keys—Discover + Connect + Take Action— demonstrate how leadership happens from the inside out. Your thoughts, enthusiasm, and approach will influence the Daisies, so take a few minutes now—and throughout the journey—to apply the three keys of leadership to yourself!

Discover	+	Connect	+	Take Action	=	Leadership

DISCOVER This journey is about the Daisies feeling confident about their ability to care for themselves and others. What abilities of yours make you feel most confident?

_____

_____

_____

CONNECT Who would you like to add to your community network in order to make this journey an enriching experience for you and the Daisies? Why do you think it's important for Daisies to meet new people and begin to expand their community network?

_____

_____

_____

TAKE ACTION How does your role as a volunteer with Girl Scout Daisies contribute to making the world better? In what ways do you believe Daisy-age girls can educate and inspire others to make the world a better place?

_____

_____

_____

Every session in this journey
has been created
to help girls become
confident leaders—
in their own lives
and in the world!

How?

The journey gets girls using
the **3 keys**
to leadership:
Discover, Connect,
and **Take Action.**

Girls
Discover
themselves.

They
Connect
with others.

And they
Take Action
in the world!

And in every session of the journey,
girls lead, team up, and learn by doing.
(And you'll learn right along with them. Have a wonderful journey!)

For more on the leadership keys and Girl Scout processes and their benefits to girls, see pages 20–21 and 110–111 in this guide, and *Transforming Leadership: Focusing on Outcomes of the New Girl Scout Leadership Experience* (GSUSA, 2008) and *Transforming Leadership Continued* (GSUSA, 2009). Both publications are available on girlscouts.org.

JOURNEY SNAPSHOT

SESSION 1
Starting Our Animal Adventure

The Daisies begin to identify ways they can care for animals. They start a Team Animal Mural and create a Team Birdbath.

SESSION 2
Caring That Counts

The Daisies explore the many ways that caring for animals is like caring for themselves. They create All About Me Nests.

SESSION 3
Tail Tales

The Daisies use their imaginations and problem-solving skills as they continue to explore how the needs of animals are similar to their own.

SESSION 4
All Creatures Great and Special

The Daisies begin to explore how animals, like people, are unique, including in the ways they communicate and move. The girls earn their Birdbath Award.

SESSION 5
Out and About with Animals

The Daisies learn more about needs of animals in preparation for teaching others about animal care.

SESSION 6
A Postcard Is Worth a Thousand Words

The Daisies continue to explore the needs of animals and use critical-thinking skills to begin to focus on specific animal needs in their community.

SESSION 7
Inspired by Animals

The Daisies continue to explore how caring for animals resembles caring for themselves. They begin their Red Robin Project to educate others about animal care.

SESSION 8
What Animals Tell Us

The Daisies strengthen their communication skills as they progress on their Red Robin Project.

SESSION 9
Teaching Others with Confidence!

The Daisies educate and inspire others on animal care with their Red Robin Project, building their own confidence along the way. They earn their Red Robin Award.

SESSION 10
Many Skills to Learn

The Daisies come to understand how caring for animals, and caring for themselves, makes them feel.

THE FINAL CELEBRATION
Celebrate Our Learning!

The Daisies celebrate what they've learned and their growing confidence in caring for animals and themselves. They earn their Tula Award.

SAMPLE SESSION 1

Starting Our Animal Adventure

SPREAD THE FUN, AND CONFIDENCE!

This first Daisy gathering can be a family kickoff event where everyone joins in to make the Team Birdbath. The Birdbath, which will hold the animal care ideas the girls learn along the journey, is a team effort that gives the girls a chance to share their skills and knowledge. The Birdbath symbolizes their ability to care for animals and their growing confidence as leaders. To publicize the kickoff, make use of the letter to the Friends and Family Network (see page 16).

FIRST-YEAR DAISIES? FIRST THINGS FIRST

If any girls in the group are new to Girl Scouting, explain that a Daisy Circle is something they form to mark these special times:

- the start of a Girl Scout Daisy gathering
- welcoming new girls and visitors
- sharing ideas
- making group decisions
- listening to the Daisy Flower Garden stories
- any time they want to talk as a group

AT A GLANCE

Goal: Daisies identify ways they can care for animals.

- Opening Ceremony: Animals Around the World (Bald Eagle: United States)
- Team Animal Mural
- Story Time: "Welcome to This Amazing Animal Adventure"
- Snack Time: Ants on a Log
- Building a Team Birdbath
- Closing Ceremony: Keeping the Girl Scout Promise

MATERIALS

- **As Girls Arrive:** copies of the girls' book, one for each girl
- **Opening Ceremony:** picture of a bald eagle, page 29; garden patches for the Daisy leadership awards, one for each girl
- **Team Animal Mural:** mural-size paper; markers, crayons, glue, and assorted craft material; a large sheet of paper and marker for jotting down the girls' ideas

- **Snack Time:** see recipe in girls' book, page 75
- **Building a Team Birdbath:** papier mâché materials (see recipe, page 32); a shallow bowl or other container, such as a pie tin and can or clay saucer and pot; colored tissue paper and other decorative materials; markers or crayons
- **Closing Ceremony:** Girl Scout Promise written on a large paper

PREPARE AHEAD

- **Chat with any assistants** about what they'll do before and during the session. Lay out or hang the paper for the Team Animal Mural. **Prepare materials** for the Team Birdbath. If using papier mâché, cover the work space with newspaper or plastic, and set out bowls for starch and paper. **Write the Girl Scout Promise** on a large sheet of paper for the Closing Ceremony.

AS GIRLS ARRIVE

Greet the girls and invite them to explore their book, especially pages 6–7, with their many hidden pictures of animals in the garden.

 ## Opening Ceremony: Animals Around the World (Bald Eagle: United States)

Gather the girls in a circle and ask them to take turns introducing themselves and naming one thing they like about animals. Start them off by saying something like: *My name is Ana. I like that my dog loves fetching a ball.*

Then let the girls know that they are about to begin an exciting Girl Scout journey about caring for animals. Say something like:

- *A journey is an adventure where you see new places, meet new people, and have lots of fun.*

- *Our journey, led by beautiful flower friends, begins in the United States.*

Show the girls the picture of a bald eagle, above right, and explain that the eagle is the national bird of the United States of America. Depending where you and the Daisies are, you might explain that the United States is the country where they live, or where they may have lived at some point in their lives.

Then ask if anyone knows the meaning of the word "national." If they don't, offer a simple explanation. If you live in the United States, you might say:

"National" means belonging to a country. The bald eagle is our national bird, just as the Stars and Stripes is our national flag.

Then share this fun fact about the bald eagle: *Bald eagles build the largest nests of any bird in North America.*

INTRODUCE THE JOURNEY'S AWARDS

The end of this Opening Ceremony is a good time to let the girls know that on this journey they will have a chance to earn three awards that show their special place as leaders in Girl Scouts. Explain that each award will be placed on a colorful garden patch, which they can wear on their Daisy tunic. Then give each girl her garden patch!

Team Animal Mural

Show the Daisies the large sheet of paper, or other art materials you've chosen, and explain that as they learn about animals on this journey, they'll team up to place each animal on their Team Animal Mural.

- Explain to the girls: *A mural is a big picture that tells a story. Usually a mural is so big, it covers a whole wall! Our mural will tell the story of all the animals we meet on this journey.*

- Guide the girls to write "Our Animal Mural" (or another title of their choice) across the top of the mural in large letters. Then invite each girl to use the art materials on hand to make one part of a bald eagle. You might say: *Let's each pick one part of the eagle to make, and then we'll put all our parts together to make one eagle! Here's what we'll need: two wings, two legs and feet, a head, body, and tail.*

- If there are more Daisies than eagle parts, suggest that the girls pair up to make a part together. Or perhaps the girls would like to make two eagles for the mural. They might even be placed at the top, one on each side of the mural's title.

As girls make their eagle parts, remind them that eagles build the largest nests in North America. Then say something like: *On this journey, you will each build a small nest during our next Daisy time together. We're going to call these nests our All About Me Nests, because they will hold all the things you know and learn about caring for yourself.* Then ask:

- *What do you have in your lives now that is like a nest?* (Answer: *Your home! Your room!*)

- *What is in your "nest"?*

Ask the girls if they have any ideas for how they would like to make and decorate their All About Me Nests, and jot their ideas on a large sheet of paper. If they don't have any ideas, suggest that they might use shoe boxes or another type of container.

TEAMING UP FOR ART AND CONFIDENCE!

Each time the girls team up for their mural or another art project, they are taking part in cooperative learning—working together toward a common goal. That means they're gaining social skills, too, such as taking turns and listening to others. And that builds confidence!

Story Time:
"Welcome to This Amazing Animal Adventure"

Introduce the journey's Flower Garden story by reading the short introduction on page 5 of the girls' book. When you finish, spark the girls' thinking by asking a few questions, like these:

- *What animals have you seen near where you live?*

- *Have you ever cared for animals in your yard or neighborhood? For example, have you ever put out a bird feeder or a birdbath?*

- *Have you ever cared for a pet, either your own or a friend's or neighbor's? What did you do? What did you like most about taking care of the pet?*

- *What is the most unusual animal you've ever seen? Where did you see it? What did it look like? Who takes care of it and how?*

After the Daisies have a chance to answer, say something like:

On this journey, you'll meet lots of animals. You'll hear how they are cared for, and how they stay safe and protected, and how they talk with one another— and you'll have a chance to care for them, too!

Engaging the Daisies in discussions, such as ones about the journey's Flower Garden stories, gives the girls opportunities to sharpen their speaking skills—and gain confidence! The ability to speak well and communicate thoughts clearly is a great leadership skill. So keep the Daisies chattering!

Snack Time!

Ants on a Log

This snack is featured on page 75 of the girls' book.
For the Daisies to make it together as a group, clean and cut celery stalks into 2- to 3-inch pieces, making enough pieces for each girl. Have cheese, hummus, or peanut butter and raisins prepared, and spoons handy to use as spreaders, so girls can decorate their logs.

MATERIALS

- Torn strips of white paper and newsprint

- Liquid starch (see recipe below)

- A shallow bowl or found/recycled container (a pie tin and can or a clay pot and saucer)

- Colored tissue paper

- Decorative materials of your choice

- Markers or crayons

TO MAKE LIQUID STARCH

1 cup cornstarch
1/2 cup cold water
1 cup boiling water

Mix the cornstarch with the cold water in a large bowl. Continue stirring as you add the boiling water to the desired consistency. (The mixture should stay clear.)

Building a Team Birdbath

If the girls will make their Team Birdbath out of papier mâché, invite the girls to the area where you've set up the papier mâché materials. Let the Daisies know that the shallow bowl (or other object) you have set out will become the birdbath, but that first they are going to cover it with papier mâché and then decorate it.

OPTION: If you and the girls prefer, simply use found or recycled materials for the Team Birdbath. Assemble them now, and get the girls decorating the birdbath with any creative materials you've gathered.

Guide the girls in dipping and soaking the torn strips of paper into the liquid starch and applying them to the bowl until it is well-covered.

- Then ask the girls to use the strips of white paper to create a final layer of papier mâché.

- Next, invite the girls to add a decorative, colored layer to the bowl using bits of colored tissue paper or other materials.

- Explain that the birdbath must now dry overnight to harden.

Then, if time allows, invite the girls to join together to create a team red robin sculpture using any remaining papier mâché materials. Let the girls know they will use the red robin sculpture in a special way during an upcoming Daisy gathering. (Turn to page 57 to see how the robin is used in Session 4's Closing Ceremony to symbolize how the girls are ready to move toward their second award, the Red Robin Award.)

**team talk!**

As the Daisies put their final touches on their Red Robin, get a discussion going about how the girls care for animals and themselves. You might get them talking with some questions, like these:

- *What are some ways people care for animals?* (Give some easy examples, if needed, such as "people feed their cats," or "people walk their dogs," and let the girls come up with more.)

- *How are these ways of caring for animals that you've mentioned similar to ways you take care of yourself?* (You might give them a few examples, such as "A cat needs food and water to live, and so do you!")

Have the girls capture their ideas about caring for animals in drawings or in words. Then invite them to put their pictures and words in the birdbath.

- Let them know that as they travel along this journey, they will continue to put their ideas into the birdbath—and they will draw ideas from it!

- Let the girls know that what they are doing is moving them toward earning their first leadership award, the Birdbath Award.

- You might also want to point the Daisies to the "Animals Need Care and So Do You" matching game on Page 78 of their book for more fun with animals and their needs.

EXTRA "TREAT" FOR EACH GIRL

The girls might enjoy using any extra papier mâché materials to create small birds or other small critters to take home. To get their imaginations soaring, ask them to think about what it might feel like to fly like an eagle or glide and leap like a dolphin, and try to capture that feeling in their sculpture.

You might point them to page 49 of their book, which features the artist Constantin Brancusi, who made sculptures of birds that seem to soar in space!

Closing Ceremony:
Keeping the Girl Scout Promise

Gather the girls around the large version of the Girl Scout Promise that you've prepared.

- Remind them—or teach them for the first time—how to make the Girl Scout sign by holding down the thumb and little finger of their right hand and extending their three middle fingers.

- Ask if anyone knows what the three fingers represent. If they don't, let them know that they symbolize the three parts of the Girl Scout Promise.

- Then get them going in a reading of the Promise. You might end by saying: *All through this journey, you'll see how the flower friends keep the Girl Scout Promise, too!*

- Now invite the Daisies to form a circle and join hands for the special Girl Scout tradition called the friendship squeeze.

- Say: *Let's cross our right arm over our left arm and hold hands with the girl on either side. Once everyone is silent, one girl starts the friendship squeeze by squeezing the hand of the girl to her left. One by one, each of you will pass on the squeeze until it travels all the way around the circle.*

Now thank the girls for a great first Girl Scout Daisy gathering, and let them know you look forward to their next time together. Encourage them to enjoy their book with their families at home, and let them know that the next time they get together, they'll hear from a special visitor who will show them how caring for animals is so much like caring for themselves.

Looking Ahead to Session 2

The Animals Safe and Sound activity makes Session 2 an ideal time for the Daisies to learn about animal safety and care from an expert visitor, such as a veterinarian, animal shelter worker, or farmer. Reach out to your Daisy Friends and Family Network for contacts and suggestions to arrange for a visit. You might also consider seeking out:

- long-term and confident pet owners in your Network

- people who take in foster/rescue pets

- staff or volunteers from the American Society for the Prevention of Cruelty to Animals or other animal organizations

- workers or volunteers at a local nature preserve or animal sanctuary

REACH OUT!

Ask your Friends and Family Network for:

☐ vegetables for the "Eat Like a Rabbit" snack (and salad dressing, a bowl, and utensils if you plan to serve the veggies salad style)

☐ paper grocery bags and decorating materials for the All About Me Nests

☐ pictures of lions so the girls can create a collage on the Team Animal Mural

WHEN SEEKING OUT POTENTIAL GUEST SPEAKERS, EXPLAIN THAT:

- Girl Scouts is a leadership experience, and for Daisies, the littlest leaders, that means learning to care for animals and themselves.

- The goal is for the Daisies to learn, firsthand from experts, about ways to care for, and be safe around, animals.

- Guest speakers will assist the girls in making an "Animals Safe and Sound" chart that lists various ways to be safe around animals (such as "Ask the owner if a pet is friendly before petting it").

- Guests are also invited to be the reader for the Daisies' Story Time!

SAMPLE SESSION 2
Caring That Counts

AT A GLANCE

Goal: Girls explore the many ways that caring for animals is like caring for themselves.

- **Opening Ceremony: Animals Around the World (Lion: Iran)**
- **Story Time: "A Purr-fect Surprise in the Garden"**
- **Animals Safe and Sound (with Guest Speaker)**
- **Snack Time: Eat Like a Rabbit**
- **All About Me Nests**
- **Closing Ceremony: Being Courageous and Strong**

MATERIALS

- **As Girls Arrive:** paper, markers, crayons, glue, craft materials

- **Opening Ceremony:** Girl Scout Law printed on a large sheet of paper; pictures of lions (one for each girl); Daisy flower friend/Girl Scout Law poster; Team Animal Mural

- **Animals Safe and Sound:** large

sheet of paper, marker, Team Birdbath

- **Snack Time:** vegetables, platter or bowl, dressing, utensils (see page 40)

- **All About Me Nests:** paper bags, decorating materials (see page 41)

PREPARE AHEAD

- Familiarize yourself with "The First Stories" chapter of the girls' book (pages 7–13) and chat with any assistants about what they'll do during the session.

- Display the Team Animal Mural, and the Girl Scout Law.

- Check that any animal expert invited to speak with the Daisies is prepared and ready to create an "Animals Safe and Sound" chart with the girls. If the expert has also agreed to read the Daisy Flower Garden story, be sure to give her time to review it.

AS GIRLS ARRIVE

Greet them and invite them to sit together and enjoy their books. Encourage each girl to use the art materials on hand to make a picture of herself doing something that shows how she takes care of herself (eating a good meal, brushing her teeth, or combing her hair). Let the girls know they'll share their pictures—and save them in a special place—when they create their own All About Me Nests later today.

 ## Opening Ceremony: Animals Around the World (Lion: Iran)

Gather the girls in a Daisy Circle and welcome them to today's Daisy session. Then introduce them to the flower friends by showing them the flower friend/ Girl Scout Law poster you have downloaded from the Girl Scout Web site or the large version you may have from the *Welcome to the Daisy Flower Garden* journey. Explain that each flower symbolizes one part of the Girl Scout Law. You might say:

- *Tula is one of the stars of our Daisy Garden story.*

- *She stands for the Girl Scout Law value of being courageous and strong.*

- *She shows that she's courageous and strong when she races after the little cat to stop it from falling into the pond.*

Then share with the girls that Tula is from the country of Holland, but her family is originally from the country of Iran. Next, show the girls a picture of a lion (you can easily use the one at right). You might say:

- *In honor of Tula, our fearless journey leader, let's take a look at the lion. Lions stand for courage, just like Tula.*

- *The lion is also a symbol of Iran, where Tula's family is from, and it is the national animal of the Netherlands, or Holland, which is Tula's homeland.*

Next, share these fun facts about lions with the girls:

- *A lion cub is born with brown spots on its body, just like the ones you see on a leopard.*

ROAR!

If any girls know more fun facts about lions, invite them to share them now. Or encourage them to describe a time they saw a lion in a zoo, on TV, in a movie, or in another place. To get them started, you might say:

A group of lions is called a "pride." What else do we know about lions?

- *As a lion cub grows up, its spots fade, but light spots often can still be seen on its legs, especially on a lioness, which is another name for a female lion.*

Invite girls to choose a picture of a lion from the stack of pictures you've gathered, and explain that they will now put their pictures together collage-style on their Team Animal Mural.

HOW MANY CRITTERS CAN YOU FIND?

The opening garden scene in the girls' book, on pages 6–7, give the Daisies a chance to search for hidden animals and insects. Encourage them to have fun finding them.

Here's a list of all of them, in case you want to give the girls some hints: bee, butterfly, cat, chipmunk, elephant, panda, robin, squirrel, turtle, woodpecker.

And here's an important hint: Some of the animals are in the clouds!

Story Time: "A Purr-fect Surprise in the Garden"

Gather the girls in a Daisy Circle and explain that in the story they are about to hear, Vi, the violet, becomes curious about a cat that wanders into the garden.

- If the girls have heard the story already, ask them what they remember.

- If they haven't, ask them what things they are curious about. Start by sharing something you are curious about, such as, "I wonder why lions lose their spots." Take turns around the circle, with each girl saying, "I am curious about . . . "

Then, read (or have a guest read) the story, and ask the girls to listen closely for the sound the cat makes. When you finish reading, get a discussion going with questions like these:

team talk!

- *Tula comforts Vi, who is a little afraid of the cat, by explaining that the cat is really nothing to fear. How do you feel when you meet a new person or a new animal?*

- *Tula explains that the cat is meowing because it is probably thirsty or tired. How do you feel when you are hungry, thirsty, or tired?*

- *The cat needs shelter, water, and food. It also needs to play and get exercise. How are your needs like the cat's needs? How are they different?*

- *The flower friends decide that it's fun to take care of the cat. Describe a time you cared for an animal or a person. How did it make you feel?*

At the end of their discussion, the girls might have fun meowing like the cat or acting out parts of the story.

Animals Safe and Sound (with Guest Speaker)

Explain to the girls that taking care of animals can certainly be fun (just as the flower friends said!), but only if we know how to keep ourselves safe. You might say:

- *Animals are not people, so they can't talk to us about their needs.*

- *Instead, they might bite or scratch as a way to tell us they are not happy or are frightened.*

- *When caring for animals, knowing how to be safe around them is very important.*

Then introduce the guest animal expert to the girls, and explain that she will tell them about her job and share some very interesting things about animal care and animal safety.

When the expert finishes talking, bring out the chart paper so that she and the girls can create an "Animals Safe and Sound" chart. Begin by drawing a line down the middle of the paper, and labeling one side "Daisies" and the other "Animals."

Then start a discussion on ways that Daisies can keep safe around animals, and write all their ideas, and ideas from the guest speaker, on the chart.

Encourage the girls to ask their guest anything they are curious about related to her work and animals. Here are some questions to get the conversation rolling:

- *What should you do to stay safe when you are playing with a cat or dog?*

- *How should you act around squirrels or chipmunks or other animals you might see in a park?*

- *Suppose you're in a dog park. How should you act toward the pets there?*

Then steer the discussion to the many ways that people can care for animals. Again, encourage the girls to ask questions, and give the expert time to answer. If you need to prompt the discussion, try to move it to ways animals can receive better care in your community. You might try some questions like these:

- *What does our community need to make life better for animals?*

- *How can we, as Daisies, help with making these things better?*

- *What's the best way to care for stray or homeless cats or dogs that we might see in our community?*

- *Why should people adopt pets from a shelter in our community?*

- *What wild animals in our community need our care, and how can we care for them?*

When the discussion wraps up, ask for a few Daisies to roll or fold up the "Animals Safe and Sound" chart and place it in the Team Birdbath.

Eat Like a Rabbit

Present the prepared platter of fresh vegetables (or salad), and let the girls know that one way to care for themselves is to eat plenty of fresh vegetables. You might say: *Think about rabbits. What do rabbits eat? Lots of vegetables!* If you are serving a salad, invite the Daisies to toss it with dressing, and serve.

GET CREATIVE!

All About Me Nests

Let the girls know that it's now time to make a nest of their own to hold all the things they know and learn along this journey that represent how they care for themselves. Keep in mind that the girls can simply start their nests now and continue decorating them the next time they get together.

- Pass out the paper bags or invite each girl to choose one. Then help them scrunch their bag into a nest shape (see photo above).

- Then invite the girls to use the craft materials on hand to decorate their nests as they like. For example, they might want to decorate the outside, and line the inside with fabric or cotton wool.

- As the girls decorate their nests, you might point out some of the fun nest facts and photos in their book (pages 14–15), and the nest photographer, Sharon Beals, featured (page 14).

- When all the girls have finished decorating, have them share the drawings they made earlier that show how they take care of themselves. Then have them place their drawings inside their All About Me Nests.

MATERIALS

- paper grocery bags (used are fine!), 1 for each girl

- assorted decorating materials (fabric, cotton wool, ribbon, glitter)

The girls' book, pages 14–15

Closing Ceremony: Being Courageous and Strong

Gather the girls in a Daisy Circle and ask them to take turns naming one thing they learned about how to care for animals from today's guest speaker. Let them know that by speaking up and asking questions, they acted strong and courageously—just like Tula, the tulip! After each girl has had a chance to speak, end the ceremony with a friendship squeeze.

Then let the Daisies know that you're looking forward to the next gathering, when each girl will share with the group another thing she does to care for herself. Ask each girl to think about what she will share, and to bring a photo or picture that represents that one way she cares for herself (for example, she might bring a picture of a hair brush, if she brushes her own hair, or a picture of a bicycle or a skate, if she gets exercise by biking or skating).

Looking Ahead to Session 3

Pourquoi [por-kwa] tales are folktales or fictional stories that tell how certain natural phenomena came to be. *Pourquoi* tales were the inspiration for the stories in the girls' book of how Red Robin and all the flowers came to have their colors. The "Spin-a-Tale" activity in the next session is a fun opportunity for the girls to have a Daisy-friendly *pourquoi* experience: They'll have a chance to express themselves creatively while thinking about animals in a new and whimsical way. To inspire the girls, you might read them some famous *pourquoi* tales, such as those listed here.

◄

Where to find *pourquoi* tales

Books

How the Leopard Got Its Spots
by Rudyard Kipling

Why Mosquitoes Buzz in People's Ears
by Verna Aardema,
illustrated by Leo and Diane Dillon

Folktale Themes and Activities for Children, Volume 1: Pourquoi Tales
by Anne Marie Kraus

Web sites
www.boop.org/jan/justso/

www.ilhawaii.net/~stony/loreindx.html

www.planetozkids.com/oban/legends.htm

If you're not able to find published stories, have some fun making up your own *pourquoi* tale. Just think of a favorite animal and create a short story about why it has some feature or characteristic. You will provide this same instruction to the girls when they create their own story. The tale can feature a sound the animal makes, a pattern in its fur, or even how it behaves (a sly fox, for example). You might even invite your Network or some teen Girl Scouts to join in the fun and really go to town with some fanciful tales.

Just begin with, "Long ago . . . " and conclude with, " . . . and that's why . . . "

REACH OUT! **Ask your Friends and Family Network for:**

☐ a recorder or video camera and technical assistance, if you'd like to record the tale the girls create in the "Spin-a-Tale" activity

☐ a CD player and music CDs that bring to mind birds and flying for the "Fly, Fly Away" activity, including various musical styles, such as classical ("The Goldfinch" from the "Spring" concerto of Vivaldi's *The Four Seasons*), pop ("Up, Up and Away" by the Fifth Dimension), '50s rock ("Rockin' Robin" by Bobby Day), and '70s rock ("Freebird" by Lynyrd Skynyrd)

☐ ingredients for the "Incredible, Edible Nests" snack

Girls gain confidence as they role-play real-life decision-making!

TAIL TALES

SAMPLE SESSION 3
Tail Tales

MAKE THE MOST OF THE GIRLS' BOOK!

As with each session along this journey, this one makes the most of the girls' book through a creative Story Time and a fun and engaging Team Talk. Notice how this Session's Team Talk focuses in on what makes each Daisy unique. Girls knowing themselves and their special skills and attributes—that's a confidence-builder, and an important part of the Discover key to leadership!

AT A GLANCE

Goal: The girls use their imagination and problem-solving skills as they continue to explore how the needs of animals are similar to their own.

- Opening Ceremony: Animals Around the World (Robin: Great Britain)

- Story Time: "The First Stories"

- Snack Time: Incredible, Edible Nests

- Spin-a-Tale

- Fly, Fly Away

- Role-Play: Choices, Choices

- Closing Ceremony: Animal-Care Ideas

MATERIALS

- **As Girls Arrive:** art and decorating materials (e.g., fabric, cotton wool, ribbon), paper, pencil

- **Opening Ceremony:** picture of a red robin, construction paper, markers, crayons, glue, and assorted craft materials; Team Animal Mural

- **Snack Time:** pretzel sticks, shredded carrots, peanut butter or yogurt cheese (see "Incredible, Edible Nests" recipe, page 75 of the girls' book)

- **Spin-a-Tale:** recording device

- **Fly, Fly Away:** strips of colored crepe paper, music, and CD player

- **Role-Play:** paper, markers, crayons, Team Birdbath

- **Closing Ceremony:** Team Birdbath

PREPARE AHEAD

- Talk with any assistants about what they'll do before and during the session.

- Review the *pourquoi* tales you've found or made up to share with the girls.

- Make streamers for the "Fly, Fly Away" activity by cutting crepe paper into arm's length strips. Have the music and CD player ready.

- Make a sample of the "Incredible, Edible Nests" snack for the girls to see when they make their own, and assemble ingredients.

AS GIRLS ARRIVE

Invite the girls to add something new to their All About Me Nests, this time a drawing or photograph brought from home of something they use to care for themselves. If they haven't brought anything, invite them to use the available art supplies to create something now.

 Opening Ceremony: Animals Around the World (Robin: Great Britain)

Have the girls gather in a Daisy Circle. Let them know that during Story Time today, they will hear more about Robin, the red robin.

- Point out that the robin is the national bird of the United Kingdom—homeland of Sunny, the sunflower, who is friendly and helpful.

- Show the girls the picture of a robin and share this fact about robins: Robins love to sing and will even sing in the middle of a cold, winter night.

- Invite girls to create a symbol of one thing the robin eats, such as worms, seeds, spiders, or other insects, and add it to the Team Animal Mural. Or, if the girls didn't make a papier mâché robin in their first gathering, have them team up to make some now out of paper or other materials you have on hand, and save one for use in the Closing Ceremony of the next session.

- After the girls have added their symbols to the mural, bring them together again in a Daisy Circle. Remind them that people need things, just as animals do. Go around the circle, and ask each girl to suggest a need people have. You might start by saying: *I need water to live. What do you need to live?*

The European robin is smaller than the American robin!

The girls' book, pages 16–17

Story Time: "The First Stories"

Today the girls will enjoy "The First Stories" chapter of their book, in which each flower friend makes up a story about how she got her color and how she's special. After reading as much of the story as you have time for today, encourage girls to discuss what makes them special. Use prompts like these to get them talking:

- *In the story today, the flower friends notice what makes them special. What's special and unique about you? Do you speak another language? Do you know magic tricks?*

- *Robin shares how she became red. Think about what you just shared about yourself, and describe how you became that way. If you speak another language, for example, how did you learn it?*

Spin-a-Tale

Invite the girls to sit in a circle. Ask who can retell the story of how Robin, the red robin, became red from today's story. Once the story has been told, explain that Robin's story is a special kind of folktale that tells why certain things in nature came to be. These folktales answer the question "Why?" but are not true stories.

You might say: "Pourquoi" *is the French word for "why," and* pourquoi *tales are old legends that explain why certain things happened, usually things having to do with animals and the natural world.*

Give some examples of some famous *pourquoi* tales, such as *How the Leopard Lost Its Spots* and *Why Mosquitoes Buzz in People's Ears.* Now start a story about how an animal got to be the way it is (such as how the zebra got its stripes) and invite the girls to continue the story, with each girl adding a new part, until they've gone all the way around the circle and made up their own *pourquoi* tale. If you are able, record the story as the girls make it up. When it is finished, make copies on DVD or in an audio file for each girl to bring or send home.

ALL FOR ONE, ONE FOR ALL

Cooperative learning—one of the three Girl Scout processes—happens when all members of a group team up toward a common goal. Structured team activities, such as "Spin-a-Tale," encourage the girls to think and create together. Each person's part is important and key to the finished product.

Snack Time!

Incredible, Edible Nests

Gather the girls around the table with your sample nest and recipe ingredients. Then invite each girl to assemble her own—and enjoy!

Fly, Fly Away

In "The First Stories," Robin shares that soon it will be time for her to fly to Mexico for the winter. Invite the girls to spread their wings and "fly" like Robin. (This can be done indoors or out.)

- Have each girl choose three streamers for each "wing."

- Then show them how to clasp the streamers together in each hand. Have them practice moving their arms up and down.

- Next, show them how to make circles or other shapes with their wings.

- When they're ready, turn on the music and invite the girls to "fly, fly away!" by dancing, skipping, running, etc., to the rhythm as they hold their crepe-paper wings at shoulder height, and let them move through the air.

- Change the music every minute or so to encourage the girls to move in time to the new beat. Invite another girl to lead the flock each time the music changes.

- For an added challenge, call out the names of birds and suggest that the girls move like each bird. (Examples: waddle like a penguin, hover like a hummingbird, run like a roadrunner, stand like a flamingo.)

Moving to music may give the girls some practice toward their Red Robin Award, which they earn farther along this journey. They might even want to present to their audience in a way that uses movement and music!

MAKE MEANING OF MUSIC

Since creativity is a theme of this journey—and that includes the music—take this opportunity to share with the girls the names of the songs and composers you used for the "Fly, Fly Away" activity. Have them share which music they liked best, and why. Also ask which they didn't like, and why.

Role-Play: Choices, Choices

Ask the girls to pair up for some role-play about making decisions.
Then read them one of these scenarios (or another that you create based on
the girls' discussions, examples from the animal expert who visited, or other
situations that have come up along the journey):

SCENARIO 1

Abby and Ellie are playing catch in Ellie's backyard when they hear a sad
little "chirp, chirp" sound coming from the woods. They follow the sound and
discover a baby bird on the ground. They look up and see the chick has fallen
from a nest in one of the trees.

"Poor little baby bird," cries Abby. "Let's get it back in its nest with its mommy,"
she suggests.

"Maybe we should go in and tell my mom," says Ellie. "I'm not sure if we should
touch it, even though it looks like it wants to get back to its nest right away."

"But the branch is so close, and the baby is so sad," says Abby.

*Take on the roles of Ellie and Abby and decide together what you will do: Lift the
bird back into its nest or tell Ellie's mom.*

SCENARIO 2

Two friends, Pilar and Jessie, are walking to a fair in their town. They are very
excited. "I'm going to go on the roller coaster!" Pilar says.

"I can't wait to play the arcade games," says Jessie.

"Yoo hoo!" calls 90-year-old Mrs. Smith from her window, as the girls pass by.
Pilar and Jessie stop. Mrs. Smith tells the girls she is not feeling well today and
asks, "Will you please walk my dog right now?"

*Take on the roles of Pilar and Jessie and decide together what you will do: Walk
the dog and be late for the fair, or tell Mrs. Smith that you can't walk her dog.*

After each pair of girls decides what they will do, have them present their
solutions to the full group of Daisies as a short role-play.

After the first scenario, you might point out that there may be other things that the girls might decide to do. For example, the girls can take the dog for a quick walk now, and a longer one after the fair. Ask if they think that might be a good thing to do.

Then wrap up by guiding the Daisies to draw pictures and write captions under them to describe how their decision to help or not help made them feel, and put them in the Team Birdbath. You might use this template. ➤

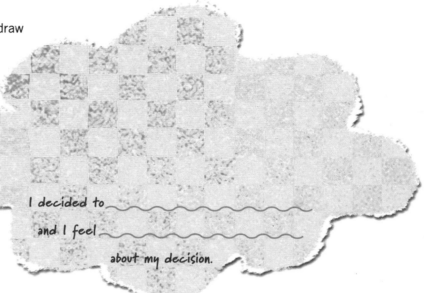

I decided to _____
and I feel _____
about my decision.

 Closing Ceremony: Animal-Care Ideas

Bring the girls together in a Daisy Circle to look at what they've put in their Team Birdbath so far. Invite each Daisy to take one paper or drawing out of the Birdbath and say what animal-care idea it represents. If a girl has trouble naming it, offer assistance.

Let girls know that the next time they get together, they'll earn their Birdbath Award, which symbolizes that they know how to care for animals and for themselves. Send them off with a big thank-you for another great session!

Looking Ahead to Session 4

Bring the Team Birdbath and enough Birdbath Awards for each girl. If you plan to ceremoniously place a robin in the Birdbath in the Closing Ceremony, bring the one the girls made in the first session or this session—or simply use a photo or drawing of a robin.

REACH OUT ▸ **Ask your Friends and Family Network for:**

- ☐ art supplies for the "Fantastical Animals Flip Book"

- ☐ ingredients for the "Apple Ladybugs" (If any girls have allergies to nuts or milk products, substitute hummus or another item for the peanut butter or yogurt cheese.)

"Fantastical Animals Flip Book"—a fantastic way to boost the Daisies' confidence!

ALL CREATURES, GREAT AND SPECIAL

SAMPLE SESSION 4
All Creatures, Great and Special

AT A GLANCE

Goal: Girls begin to explore how animals, like people, are unique, including in the ways they communicate and move.

- Opening Ceremony: Animals Around the World (Cheetah: Kenya)

- Earning the Birdbath Award

- Story Time: "The First Stories" (continued)

- Fantastical Animals Flip Book

- Snack Time: Apple Ladybugs

- Busy Squirrels Song and Dance

- Closing Ceremony: Moving Toward the Red Robin Award

MATERIALS

- **Opening Ceremony:** picture of a cheetah (page 51), markers, crayons, glue, assorted craft materials; Team Animal Mural

- **Earning the Birdbath Award:** Birdbath Awards (one for each girl); girls' books

- **Fantastical Animals Flip Book:** construction paper or thin cardboard; three-ring binder; animal pictures of approximately

the same size cut from magazines; glue sticks; scissors; hole punch; and (if girls will draw their own animals) crayons, markers, colored pencils, and other craft materials

- **Snack Time:** (see "Apple Ladybugs" recipe, page 74 in the girls' book)

- **Closing Ceremony:** the robin the girls have made or any image of a robin; Team Birdbath

PREPARE AHEAD

- Set out the art supplies for the "Fantastical Animals Flip Book."

- Core and slice apples in half from top to bottom for the "Apple Ladybugs," and prepare other ingredients the girls will need to make them (see page 74 in the girls' book). Make certain about peanut and/or dairy allergies before choosing the toppings.

 ## Opening Ceremony: Animals Around the World (Cheetah: Kenya)

Gather the girls in a Daisy Circle and say something like: *During the flower friends' story, "A Purr-fect Surprise in the Garden," Mari, the marigold, says that on her travels, she's seen many cats, big and small.*

- Point out that the cheetah, a big cat, is the national animal of Kenya, a country in Africa, Mari's homeland.

- Show the girls the picture of a cheetah, below, and share these facts, some of which the girls may have already learned from their book:

The cheetah is the fastest mammal on land. It can move as fast as 70 miles an hour! That is like a very fast car moving on the highway or a racetrack!

- Then let them know that cheetahs, like other wild animals, need plenty of space for exercise.

Invite the girls to create a cheetah for their Team Animal Mural. Let them know that their cheetahs don't have to look exactly like the picture of the cheetah that you showed them. Maybe they want to draw how a cheetah feels when it runs at top speed or when it rests in the shade after a fast run. (And since Mari says she's seen "many cats," give the girls the option of drawing or making as many cats as they wish—big and little!)

> **CHEETAH IN ACTION**
>
> If you have access to the Internet, you might show the girls a video clip of a cheetah in action at http://kids.nationalgeographic.com/Animals/CreatureFeature/Cheetah.

Earning the Birdbath Award

Ask the girls to come together in a circle, and let them know they have earned their Birdbath Award, which represents that they can say, "Animals need care; I need care. I can do both." Invite them to go around the circle and say one way they can care for animals and one way they can care for themselves.

Complete the ceremony by giving each girl a Birdbath Award. Congratulate them on earning their first leadership award on the journey! Encourage any older Daisies to help the younger ones.

Then urge the girls to continue caring for animals, and to keep adding ideas to their Team Birdbath all along the journey.

Story Time: "The First Stories" (continued)

Continue reading "The First Stories," in which Robin and the flower friends tell how they came to have their colors.

After the girls hear the story, encourage them to make up their own story about how their Girl Scout Daisy tunics came to be the color blue. You might say something like:

- *Most daisies are white and yellow, but the Daisy tunic is blue. How do you think the Daisy tunic got its color? Could it be because Daisies love to be under the blue sky? Or maybe they sailed across the blue sea?*

- *Let's make up a story! Let's start our story by saying, "One day, long ago in a beautiful garden . . . "*

Then, invite the girls to go around the circle, taking turns adding a sentence of their own to the story.

Fantastical Animals Flip Book

MATERIALS

- construction paper or thin cardboard
- three-ring binder
- animal pictures of approximately the same size cut from magazines
- glue sticks
- scissors
- hole punch, crayons, markers, colored pencils, and other craft materials (if girls will draw their own animals)

Introduce this team-building art activity by reminding the girls that all animals—like all people—are special in their own way. You might also say that all animals are unique.

Ask if any girls know what *unique* means. If they aren't sure (or their answers aren't quite on target!), let them know that *unique* means interesting, special, cool, and different all rolled into one. You might say:

Animals are unique, and so are all Daisies! (The girls may even know the TV character Uniqua from the children's TV show "The Backyardigans.")

Let the girls know that they're going to team up to make a flip book of unique animals—animals they make up! They're going to see firsthand how cool it is to be unique.

Depending on how you've decided to structure this activity, ask each girl to:

A. Choose an animal picture from the selection you have and paste it on a sheet of cardboard or construction paper,

OR

B. Draw an animal of their choice on the paper you provide.

If the girls are drawing their animals, make sure they all create their drawings in the same way—either horizontally or vertically—and roughly the same size. You might have the girls draw the head on the right side of the paper, the front legs in the middle, and the hind legs and tail on the left. Be sure to encourage any older Daisies to help the younger ones!

- When the girls finish, work with them to make their team flip book.

- First, have them each cut their animal into three parts: head, body, legs/feet.

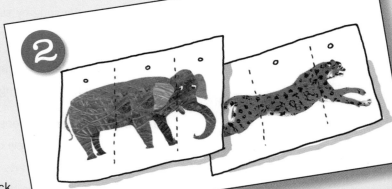

- Using a hole punch, have the girls make one hole in each of the three "body part" sections, making sure to line them up with the rings of the binder.

- Then, place the three parts of each girl's animal in the binder.

- Now, the girls are ready to flip the pages back and forth to create new and wondrous animals (rabbit's head/giraffe's body/duck's feet—whatever combination can be created from their pictures).

Once the girls have flipped through the book to enjoy all the "Fantastical Animals," get them talking about their creations and what they see in them, using questions such as these:

team talk!

- *Which flip-book animal is your favorite? What name would you give it?*

- *What could an animal with a rabbit's head, a giraffe's body, and a duck's feet be good at?*

Then get the girls thinking about these important questions:

- **Why is it good for animals to be different from one another?**

- **Why is it good for people to be different from one another?**

Wrap up the discussion by inviting the girls to take turns saying one thing about themselves that makes them feel unique. Go around once more, with each girl stating something she learned about another Daisy that she thinks is interesting or cool, and why.

Busy Squirrels Song and Dance

Get the girls up and moving for the "Busy Squirrels Song and Dance," which underscores the idea that animals need food, exercise, and rest. Introduce the song by singing or chanting it yourself while imitating a squirrel searching, digging, and storing nuts for winter.

Any animal and its actions can be added to create more verses: birds looking for worms, chipmunks looking for berries, dogs looking for bones, and so on.

Next, invite each girl to choose an animal to use in a new version of the song. Each girl repeats with a new critter in the garden, acknowledging what the animal needs and finds in its natural setting. After each girl has had a chance to imitate an animal, have them review all the critters' needs and discuss how they, as Daisies, might provide for those needs.

team talk!

Then get the girls thinking about the stories they've just told, and the pride and confidence they can take from that. Say something like:

- *You've just told a story through song and dance! How else have you told stories on this journey? (Answers: pictures, words, sculpture, the flip book.)*

- *What have you tried on this journey that you had never done before? How does it feel to try something new?*

- *What ways of telling stories would you like to try more of? What new ways would you like to try?*

Snack Time!

Apple Ladybugs

Show the girls the picture and recipe for "Apple Ladybugs" in their book. Then set out the apple slices and other ingredients and guide the girls in making the snack. Then enjoy!

Telling stories through song and dance gives the girls some practice toward their Red Robin Award—they may want to present to their audience in a way that uses movement and music!

Closing Ceremony: Moving Toward the Red Robin Award

Bring out the papier mâché robin the girls created during their first gathering (Session 1) and gather the girls around their Team Birdbath. Let them know that this red robin is a symbol of how they will fly out, just like a robin, to teach others about the importance of caring for animals. Then ask them, together as a team, to place their red robin into the Birdbath ceremoniously, to show how they are now ready to move forward toward earning their next leadership award, the Red Robin Award. Let them know they'll start doing that the very next time they gather!

IF YOU ARE PLANNING A FIELD TRIP FOR SESSION 5: Before the girls leave, let them know that the next time they get together, they will be taking a field trip to see how animals receive care. Say something like:

You'll be going to a new place, meeting animals, and learning new things—just like the flower friends on their travels!

Engage the girls in a quick brainstorm of questions about animal care that they would like answers to, especially ones about animal-care needs in their community. Jot down each question and the name of the Daisy who asked it, so that you can remind the girls during the field trip.

Then invite the Daisies to enjoy their books at home, and let them know you look forward to their next time together.

The Busy Squirrels Song

There once were some ver—y bus—y squirrels . . . (Clap hands twice)
(Hands on hips, bend and straighten knees as singing)

Work—ing hard in the gar—den all day . . . (Clap hands twice)
(Hands on hips, bend and straighten knees as singing)

Gath — er — ing a — corns . . .
(Bend and scoop up nuts as singing)

They still had time to play!
(Turn head side to side as if saying "NO")

They skipped all a — round . . .
(Skip through space)

They stopped . . .   They found a — corns!
(Stop, look of surprise)

They scooped them up . . .
(Pretend to dig with paws)

And then they looked for more!
(Hand to forehead as if searching)

Words by Alice Carpenter

Music by Peter Capucilli

They skipped all a — round . . .
(Skip through space)

They stopped . . .
(Stop, look of surprise)

They found more acorns!

They scooped them up . . .
(Pretend to dig with paws)

And looked a — round a — gain!
(Hand to forehead as if searching)

Their acorns were ver — y heav — y . . .
(Pretend to hold heavy armful of acorns, swing arms side to side)

Let's go back to the nest . . .
(Skip again, more slowly)

Let's put them in a hid — ing place . . .
(Pretend to dig and cover acorns)

And now the squirrels take a rest!
(Squirrels yawn, curl up on the ground, and pretend to sleep)

Looking Ahead to Session 5

Session 5 is a good time for the girls to see animal care firsthand. With assistance from your Network, arrange a visit to a farm, animal shelter, veterinary office, or any other place where animals receive care. This trip lets the girls gather animal-care ideas to teach others, and, by getting out and about, they are able to connect with their community—one of the national Girl Scout leadership outcomes. This also moves them forward with earning their Red Robin Award. Be sure to bring the girls' questions from their Session 4 brainstorm.

Also reach out to your Network for assistance in arranging any needed transportation and chaperones, or reach out to older Girl Scouts who have an interest in animals to accompany the Daisies.

TALKING POINTS — **When speaking with potential hosts for the Daisies, explain that:**

☐ Girl Scouts is a leadership experience, and for Daisies, our littlest leaders, that means learning to care for animals and themselves.

☐ The visit will let the girls learn firsthand about the many ways people care for animals and how that care resembles the care the girls give themselves.

If a field trip can't be arranged, call on your Network to borrow some books and DVDs on animal care to share with the Daisies, or arrange to show the girls some animal care Web sites, such as those suggested below.

Animal-Care Resources

Books

A Day in the Life of a Veterinarian
by Heather Adamson.
Capstone Press, August 2000.

A Kids' Guide to Protecting & Caring for Animals: How to Take Action
by Cathryn Berger Kaye.
Free Spirit Publishing, August 2008.

Farmers and Ranchers Care About Their Animals
by Dan Yunk.
Dan Yunk, May 2009.

DVDs

Discovery Education: When I Grow Up I Want To Be a Veterinarian
http://store.discoveryeducation.com/product/show/53888

Web sites

http://content.scholastic.com/browse/article.jsp?id=3746688

http://teacher.scholastic.com/commclub/vet/

http://teacher.scholastic.com/wolves/vet.htm

http://vetmedicine.about.com/od/veterinarycareers/a/VVP_animalcare.htm

OPTION: Consider taking the girls on a "Sounds of Nature Walk" at a nature preserve, at the seashore, by a lake, or at a park near your meeting place. Even a stroll in the neighborhood will do. Plan to take along a recording device to capture any animal sounds the girls hear.

Understanding body language— that's a great social skill and confidence-builder!

OUT AND ABOUT WITH ANIMALS

SAMPLE SESSION 5
Out and About with Animals

AT A GLANCE

Goal: Girls learn more about the day-to-day needs of animals in preparation for teaching others about animal care.

- Opening Ceremony
- Field Trip
- Option: Sounds of Nature Walk

- Animals Talk and So Do We!
- Closing Ceremony

MATERIALS

- **Sounds of Nature Walk:** recorder
- **Role-Play:** paper, markers, crayons, glue, and assorted craft materials; Team Animal Mural

Opening Ceremony

If the Daisies are meeting at a new place, simply form a circle and ask each girl to name one thing that's special about where they are now. Then:

- Remind the girls about the Girl Scout Law line, "Respect myself and others." Ask: *How can we show respect during our field trip today?*

- You can say that listening closely to their host is one way to show respect.

Field Trip

Introduce the girls to their host, who will share her work and take questions from the girls.

When the time for questions comes, prompt the girls using their questions from the brainstorm they engaged in during the last session. Use the animal-care worker's expertise to find ways that people in your community can care for animals, so the girls can educate and inspire others about them.

Option: Sounds of Nature Walk

Before heading out on the walk, remind the girls that every animal has its own way of communicating, just as humans have their way. Invite the girls to brainstorm the many ways they communicate. Prompt the discussion by asking questions such as:

- *How might you show that you are sad or happy?*

- *How many ways do you communicate with your family?* (Possible answers: talk face-to-face, phone, gestures, facial expressions.)

- *How might someone who cannot hear communicate?*

team talk!

Point out that, since animals can't talk like people, they use sounds and actions to communicate. Then ask the girls to brainstorm animal sounds they've heard. For fun, encourage them to imitate those sounds.

As the girls walk, encourage them to listen carefully to the sounds of nature, specifically animals—from a dog's bark to the buzzing of an insect. As they hear a sound, ask them to call it out to the rest of the group. (If this gets too chaotic, suggest that girls raise their hands to share what they hear.) If you can, record the sounds the girls hear on the walk, so they can listen to them again when they are back at their Daisy meeting place.

ROLE-PLAY: WHAT ANIMAL AM I?

After their nature walk, get the Daisies talking about the sounds they heard. If you recorded the sounds, play them back now, and have the girls try to identify the animal that made each one.

Then invite the girls to gather in a Daisy Circle, and one at a time, ask each girl to imitate an animal she saw and/or heard, while the rest of the girls try to guess the animal and what it is trying to "say."

Then ask the girls to pair up to act out a scene of an animal doing something or wanting something. As each pair presents, the rest of the girls will guess the animals in it and what they are doing or "saying." Below are scenarios to suggest if the girls don't readily think up their own (just be sure you give the scenario to each pair privately, so the rest of the group won't know it!):

- **a person playing fetch with a dog** (Girls might guess that it's a dog playing fetch, and that the dog is communicating that it wants its owner to throw the ball.)

- **a bird singing** (from a birdhouse, birdcage, windowsill, or porch) to a bird in the wild (Girls might guess the animals are birds and are chatting with each other about where to find food.)

- **a blind person walking with a seeing-eye dog** (Girls might guess that the dog is guiding the blind person.)

After every girl or pair has performed, and if time allows, invite the Daisies to draw pictures of animals they heard or saw on their walk to add to their Team Animal Mural. If you captured sound recordings of the animals, the girls may have fun playing the recording as they draw.

Animals Talk and So Do We

If the girls have time after their field trip or nature walk, get started on this confidence-building activity by asking the girls to recall some of the many ways animals communicate. (If time is short, save this important activity for another day!) To get them talking, toss out a few simple examples, such as dogs bark and birds chirp. If you can, use examples from animals the girls have just seen (or heard) on their field trip or their nature walk. You might say something like:

- *Just like animals, we use our voices to communicate.*

- *We talk to share ideas and express how we feel. But talking is not the only way we communicate.*

- *We use our bodies every day, and every day we use our bodies in many ways to communicate.*

- *If you see someone yawn, what does that tell you about her?*

- *If you see someone jumping up and down and smiling, what does that tell you about how she is feeling?*

● *What does it mean when you shake your head up and down? What about when you move your head from side to side?*

team talk! Now ask each girl to take a turn "saying" something to the group by using only her body and not any words. You might say:

Tell us something by how you stand or sit or walk. Or tell us something by the expression on your face. As each of you tries to tell us something with your body, the rest of us will guess what you are trying to "say."

Consider starting them off with an example: You might walk around the room dragging your feet to show you are tired or sad. Ask: *Can any of you guess what I'm trying to say?*

After all the girls have had a turn, get them talking about how their "body language" can sometimes actually change the way they feel. Point out that sometimes, if they act a certain way, such as dragging their feet or slumping their shoulders, they might actually feel more tired or sadder. And sometimes, just smiling and laughing can make everyone feel better!

With this in mind, ask the Daisies to all jump up and smile and laugh for a minute. When they're done, ask: *So, how do you feel? Energized and happy about all you've been learning about animals and all that you can do to care for them?*

Point the girls to the "Tell a Story Without Words!" matching game on page 48 in their book for more fun with body language.

Matching game,
girls' book, page 48

 Closing Ceremony

Gather the girls in a circle and end this Daisy time with a simple friendship squeeze.

Looking Ahead to Session 6

In the next session, the girls will use materials to represent a donkey on the Team Animal Mural. Gather or reach out to the Network for remnants of fake fur, felt, or other fabrics for the donkey's body; straw, yarn, or corn silk for the tail; chamois or dried sponge for the nose, or other materials. Or, if you prefer to keep things simple, the girls can team up to draw a donkey or create a collage using images of donkeys from magazines or other sources.

Also reach out to your Network for poster board or card stock cut into postcard–size rectangles for "The Power of a Postcard" activity, and for snacks, either apples for apple "smiles" or kabobs, or cheese and tortillas for quesadillas.

A Postcard Is Worth a Thousand Words

CARING LEADS TO CONFIDENCE!

The "Comparing the Caring" activity in this session gets the Daisies using critical-thinking skills and connecting with their community. Critical thinking is part of the Discovery key, and connecting with their community is, of course, part of the Connect key. And by seeing all they're learning, the Daisies gain confidence!

AT A GLANCE

Goal: The girls continue to explore the needs of animals and begin to focus in on specific animal needs in their communities.

- Opening Ceremony: Animals Around the World (Donkey: Mexico)
- Story Time: "Zinni's Story"
- The Power of a Postcard
- Snack Time: Apple Snacks or Quesadillas
- Comparing the Caring
- Closing Ceremony: Sharing the Caring
- Preparing for the Red Robin Project

MATERIALS

- **As Girls Arrive:** girls' books
- **Opening Ceremony:** picture of donkey (page 69 in this guide and page 32 in the girls' book); fabric scraps and other materials for making a donkey
- **The Power of a Postcard:** postcards or postcard-size pieces of card stock, markers, crayons, and assorted craft materials
- **Snack Time:** ingredients for apple "smiles" or kabobs, or quesadillas (see recipes, page 72)
- **Comparing the Caring:** large sheet of paper, marker, Team Birdbath

PREPARE AHEAD

- Talk with any assistants about what they'll do before and during the session.

- In preparation for "Comparing the Caring," create a three-column chart on a large sheet of paper. Label the left column "Flower Friends," the middle column "Discussion," and the right column "Animal Experts." Put the title, "Comparing the Caring," at the top.

- Create postcard-size rectangles from poster board or card stock for each girl, if not already prepared.

- Cut the apples into slices or chunks, depending on which snack you will be serving; or, if you have cooking facilities and plan to make quesadillas, set out the grated cheese and tortillas.

AS GIRLS ARRIVE

Welcome the girls as they arrive, and invite them to enjoy their books, especially the picture puzzle on page 48, where they try to figure out what the flower friends are feeling.

 ## Opening Ceremony: Animals Around the World (Donkey: Mexico)

Gather the girls in a Daisy Circle and let them know that today they will hear about how Zinni visits a farm in Mexico, and how proud she feels when she cares for animals.

Show the picture of a donkey and say something like:

- *If we were in Mexico with Zinni, one animal we might see is the donkey, which is called a* burro *in Spanish. Who can share something they know about the donkey?* (Give girls a chance to respond. If they don't know, share with them that donkeys often help people carry things, just as they'll hear about in "Zinni's Story.")

- Then share these fun facts about donkeys:

     Donkeys are related to horses and zebras.
     Donkeys are slower than and not as strong as horses, but they are very smart.

Invite girls to touch the fake fur or felt, straw, and other materials, and imagine how it would feel to pet a donkey. Then invite the Daisies as a team to make those materials into a donkey for their Team Animal Mural.

THE POWER OF STORIES

Storytelling through words and pictures is a powerful way to share ideas, thoughts, and feelings, and a creative skill that helps Daisies develop a strong sense of self. Sharing stories also develops healthy relationships among the girls while empowering them to connect with their Girl Scout community and beyond.

Story Time: "Zinni's Story"

Today the girls will enjoy "Zinni's Story," in which she shares her visit to Mexico through pictures from her photo album. She hears roosters and cows, and meets a horse and a chick.

team talk!

After the girls hear the story, get a discussion going with questions like these:

- *At the end of the story we heard today, Gloria receives a postcard. Whom have you received postcards from before?*

- *If you could send a postcard to someone today, who would it be?*

Then launch right into the postcard-making activity on the opposite page.

A VISIT TO THE POST OFFICE

Visiting your neighborhood post office, and perhaps arranging a tour of its inner workings, offers a great opportunity for girls to connect with their community—one of the national Girl Scout leadership outcomes. Before you go, brainstorm with the girls a list of things to ask and look for on their visit!

SNAIL MAIL VERSUS E-MAIL

You might take a minute or two to talk with the girls about how mail from the post office is now known as "snail mail" because, like a snail, mail delivery by postal workers is much slower than e-mail, which can arrive in your computer inbox in seconds. You might ask:

- *Have you ever sent or received an e-mail? Or have you seen family members send and receive e-mail?*

- *What would you rather receive, an e-mail or a piece of snail mail? Why?*

ANIMALS AS MAIL CARRIERS

You might also share these fun facts about mail with the Daisies:

Before the invention of trains and planes, animals delivered the mail! It's true. Pigeons, called carrier pigeons, carried messages from one place to another. And the Pony Express was made up of mail carriers on horseback! It took 10 days for them to deliver the nation's mail from Missouri to California. Imagine!

PONY EXPRESS · SAN FRANCISCO · AUG. 1

USA

......postcard......

To:

Address:

The Power of a Postcard

Let the girls know that they will now have a chance to make some picture postcards like the one Gloria talks about in "Zinni's Story." Explain that rather than drawing pictures of a trip, they can create a picture that shows one important way to care for animals. To get them thinking of what to put on their postcard, remind them of all the animal-care ideas they now have in the Team Birdbath.

Then give each girl a postcard or postcard-size piece of card stock. Using whatever creative materials you have on hand, have them draw their animal-care idea on one side of the card.

On the other side, assist the girls in creating a sentence that explains their picture. For example, *If you own a cat, be sure to feed it each day.* Then work with the girls to address the postcards to a friend or family member.

When the girls are ready, have them share their postcards, and the animal-care ideas they feature, with one another. Wrap up by pointing out how sending or passing along a postcard is a good way to spread the word about caring for animals! And be sure to ask: *And when you spread the word about good things to do, what are you being?* (Answer: A leader!)

THE POWER OF A POSTCARD, PART 2

If the girls enjoy making postcards, they can use what they've learned as part of their Red Robin Project. They can show the cards they've created, and then invite their audience members to make their own postcards about an animal-care idea they've just learned from the Daisies. Just plan to have the postcard materials on hand so that audience members can join in immediately to make postcards that they send to their friends and others, thus ensuring that the Daisies' animal-care message goes viral! (Look ahead to page 91 for how this plays out in Session 9.)

Snack Time!

Apple Snacks

Make apple "smiles" and sprinkle them with a little cinnamon, or make apple kabobs using wooden skewers and small chunks of apples alternated with grapes, blueberries, or other berries. Allow about half an apple or two kabobs per girl.

Quesadillas

Use whole-wheat tortillas and grated cheddar cheese. Heat the tortilla in a heavy skillet, and sprinkle a scant handful of cheese on the tortilla. When the cheese begins to melt, fold the tortilla in half, and finish cooking. Transfer to a cutting board and cut into wedges.

Serve the snack, and as the girls enjoy it, start a discussion about how it feels to make and enjoy a healthy snack for themselves, and how eating healthful foods is a way they can care for themselves. To get things rolling, you might ask:

- *In the story, Zinni and her family eat some vegetables with their quesadillas. What were they?*
- *What foods do you like to eat?*
- *How does eating fresh vegetables make you feel?*

SAY "NO" TO YES/NO QUESTIONS

To keep discussions lively, ask open-ended questions that allow for lots of rich conversation. Avoid questions that the girls can answer with a simple "yes" or "no." Notice how the bulleted questions throughout this guide can't be answered with "yes" or "no." For example, you wouldn't ask, "Have you ever cared for an animal?" Instead, you might ask, "How have you cared for an animal?"

Comparing the Caring

The "Comparing the Caring" chart will help the girls focus on animal needs in their community to present to their audience. In doing so, they'll use critical-thinking skills and connect with their community—two national Girl Scout leadership outcomes. And by seeing all they're learning, they'll gain confidence.

Display the chart and gather the girls in front of it. Begin by pointing out the many ways they've learned to care for animals along the journey. In the story, they heard about how the flower friends take care of animals. In Daisy discussions, they've shared a little about how they care for animals, and they've met animal experts who care for animals, too.

team talk!

Begin with the flower friends. Ask questions, like the ones below, about how the flower friends have cared for animals. Jot their answers on the chart.

- *What animal do the flower friends care for at the beginning of the story?*
- *What does the animal need? How do the flower friends care for it?*
- *How does caring for the animal make the flower friends feel?*
- *How does Zinni care for animals in Mexico? How does this make her feel?*

Next, ask questions such as these about the girls' own caring for animals. Jot their responses on chart paper.

- *Who in our Daisy group has cared for animals? How has she cared for them?*

- *How has caring for animals made us feel?*

Remind the girls about the animal expert who spoke to them about animal safety. Ask what they remember about how she cared for animals in a safe way. Write their responses in the last column. If they went on a field trip, you might ask:

- *What kind of animals did we see?*

- *What did the animals need? Who takes care of these needs? How?*

- *How does caring for the animals make this person feel? How can you tell?*

When the chart is complete, guide the girls to notice similarities and differences. To get the discussion going, ask questions such as:

- *What needs do all these animals have? What needs do only some of them have?*

- *How is caring for all animals the same? How is it different for some?*

- *How does caring for animals make people (and flower friends!) feel?*

Explain to the girls that at the next gathering, they will start to put together a project about caring for animals—their "story" of animal care!—that they will ultimately present to others in their community. Point out that this chart is their first step in thinking about what story they will tell. Ask the girls to each name their favorite idea from the chart, and record their answers for use at their next gathering. Then ask one or more of the Daisies to fold or roll up the chart and put it in the Team Birdbath.

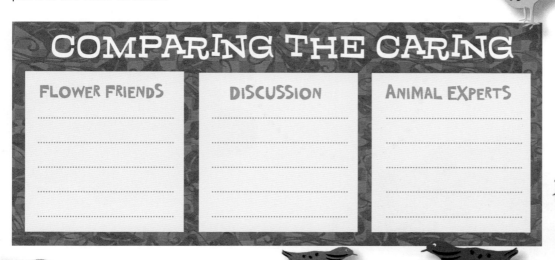

COMPARING THE CARING

FLOWER FRIENDS	DISCUSSION	ANIMAL EXPERTS

Closing Ceremony: Sharing the Caring

Gather the girls in a Daisy Circle, and invite them to take turns naming one thing they want to share with others about caring for animals. Let the girls know that they'll consider all these ideas, and all the ideas in their "Comparing the Caring" chart, as they move toward earning their Red Robin Award. Then close the gathering with a friendship squeeze.

Encourage the girls to enjoy their book between sessions. Point them to pages 72–73 and 76–77, so they can learn about four young women who care for animals—and some animals that care for people, too! Let the Daisies know that you look forward to the group's next time together.

Girls' book, pages 72–73

Looking Ahead to Session 7

Girls will do some "Japanese Garden Yoga" during the next session. You might want to find some soft, calming music to play for them. They'll also begin preparing their Red Robin Project during the next session. Use the following preparation tips and project pointers as needed to keep the girls on track.

Red Robin Project Planner

Preparing for the Red Robin Project

The Red Robin Award recognizes that girls can fly out into the world just like Robin, the red robin, to teach others about caring for animals. So for the next several gatherings, you'll be guiding the girls to plan what new knowledge they want to share with others, how they will share it, and with whom.

Keep in mind the Daisies' teaching doesn't have to be elaborate to have an impact. Their audience doesn't have to be big, either. What's most important is that the Daisies have the confidence-building experience of teaching others and have fun "telling the story" of what they've learned. So use the tips on these pages to guide the Daisies' efforts.

As you guide the girls to zero in on what they will teach, also assist them in choosing a creative way to teach it. Make use of all the learning and art the Daisies have done along the journey. Take your cues from the girls, and make use of all the ideas of animal caring they listed on their "Comparing the Caring" chart in Session 6. The following examples of Red Robin Project ideas will make the most of journey activities and get you and the girls thinking.

CHECK LIST

A successful Red Robin Project gives girls an opportunity to:

☐ Meet new people.

☐ Have fun sharing what they've learned along their journey.

☐ Use one (or more!) creative ways to tell stories that they've explored (song, dance, postcard, mural, etc.).

☐ Ask their audience to spread the word about caring for animals, too.

ANIMAL-CARE FAIR

If the girls enjoyed a range of the activities and animal-care ideas along the journey, they might present them at various "booths" set up like a fair or exhibit, where the audience can roam from booth to booth, as Daisies at each station talk about one small tip for animal care, such as a grooming tip, a feeding tip, or an exercise tip.

ANIMAL-CARE MURAL

If making their Team Animal Mural and drawing excited them, they might create a new mural in panels or make posters or a team scrapbook to show the animal-care ideas they want to share with their audience. They might even give their audience copies of what they create.

PERFORMANCE OR DANCE

If they loved the "Busy Squirrels Song and Dance" and "Fly, Fly Away" activities, they might enjoy making up and performing a dance that dramatizes an animal-care idea.

ARTS AND CRAFTS

If they enjoy arts and crafts, they might want to take photographs to create a photo story, or they might use their papier mâché birds and other critters to tell about an animal-care issue.

OTHER IDEAS

....
....
....
....

If you have other ideas, go for it! Just keep in mind the time you have available and whom it is possible to gather for the Daisies' "audience."

Identify and Reach Out to an Audience

Once you and the girls have settled on what to teach and how to teach it, it's time to choose an audience the girls would like to inspire.

- A good audience doesn't have to be large. Five or six interested folks will do! They might be siblings of the Daisies, or a few teachers or PTA members who agree to add a half-hour to a meeting. What's important is that the audience is made up of active listeners—people who will hear what the Daisies say and pass it on!

- Encourage the girls and your Network to talk about who would be the right audience. Any experts the girls have visited may also have recommendations.

- Keep in mind that, depending on the situation, either what the Daisies are teaching will determine their audience, or their audience will determine what they teach! For example, animal-safety tips might be an appropriate message for an audience of younger children; the importance of adopting pets from a shelter or putting ID tags on pets might be a good lesson for families or neighborhood groups. If the Daisies are presenting to preschoolers, they might "tell" their story in a simpler way, too, than if teaching a group of adults.

Audience ideas:

- a preschool group (that way, the Daisies will be the "big kids"!)

- a group of Daisies from another area

- family members and friends or people from their neighborhood

- animal-care organization

- their school, either as part of a class or during a lunch period

- a Sunday school or other religious class

- an existing after-school program

Tap your Network for help

If Network members teach or volunteer at preschool, after-school programs, or places of worship, or if some belong to a block group, tap them for ideas on audiences or locations where the girls can present.

If you're inviting adults, you might let them know that this is an opportunity for the Daisies to gain confidence and leadership skills and to meet new people, and that their attendance can help the girls grow!

NO LIVE AUDIENCE POSSIBLE?

Make and share a video or simple booklet that features the girls' story of their learning!

6

A POSTCARD IS WORTH A THOUSAND WORDS

Red Robin Project Planner

RED ROBIN PROJECT PLANNING CHECKLIST

Choose one (or more) animal-care ideas as the basis for the girls' teaching.

☐ Use the Team Birdbath and/or the "Comparing the Caring" chart for ideas, and brainstorm with the girls and your Network, or use your discretion.

☐ Keep in mind that what Daisies teach can be simple safety tips, such as asking if it's safe before petting a dog you don't know; simple Do-It-Yourself projects, such as making a bird feeder; or regional issues, such as the importance of preserving open spaces for birds and wild animals.

Add some creativity to the Daisies' teaching!

☐ Consider which activities the girls have enjoyed along the journey, and what time and resources allow.

- If the Daisies will host a series of animal-care stations, make use of any or all the creative mediums they have explored along the journey and those they explore in Sessions 7 and 8: photos, murals, drawings, papier mâché, posters, etc.

- If they will teach their audience by using a "story" that they speak or perform, consider enhancing the telling with a puppet show, dance, or play; or by making and sharing a book of the story; or by creating an exhibition, fair, mural, or photo show-and-tell; or simply by taking turns telling parts of the story.

Keep in mind that what the Daisies teach and *what form* they teach it in are not nearly as important as the fact that the project gives the girls the opportunity to see for themselves that they have knowledge to share with others!

Make use of activities already built into the Sample Sessions.

For example, if you choose to do an exhibit or fair, use activities such as "Busy Squirrels Song and Dance" (Session 4), "Comparing the Caring" chart (Session 6), and "The Power of a Postcard, Part 2" (Session 6) for exhibits. Use the "Animal Riddle Poem" (Session 7) as an icebreaker for the crowd. Or girls can simply pick one animal-care tip from their Team Birdbath and an object to represent it, and talk about it. (For example, "It's important for cats to have fresh water," and a water bowl. A girl can talk about her own pet, the cat in the flower story, a cat she saw at the vet, etc.)

Decide how much time you, the Daisies, and your Network can spend—and plan accordingly.

If you have just one session for planning and one for presenting, that's fine. Just offer a few stations or displays or a short show. If you have more time, the girls can set their imaginations and creativity free and do something more elaborate. And perhaps they can add some teaching on the Girl Scout Promise and Law! Either way, let the girls use teamwork and take the lead in planning what they want to say and do.

Red Robin Project Planner

Use this template to create invitations for the Daisies' audience:

Join Our Littlest Leaders as They Tell Their Story of Animal Care!

Please join us on ....

at ....

to hear our Daisy group, ...,

teach about the importance of animal care.

As the Daisies share what they've learned, they are also achieving some of the important leadership benefits of Girl Scouting. They are connecting with their community and gaining a great sense of themselves as leaders who can make the world a better place.

This gives the girls a great sense of confidence in all they do!

☐ **Use these "script starters" to create speaking points for the girls:**

Script Starter for the Red Robin Project

> **Daisy Announcer:** Today our Daisy group will share with you important ways to care for animals and invite you to keep animals safe and sound, and teach others how to do that, too!
>
> **Daisies in unison:** "To keep animals safe and sound, it's important to
>
> _____
>
> _____
>
> _____."
>
> **Following their presentation, the girls say:**
>
> Will you join us in pledging to do your best to keep animals safe and sound? If you do, will you keep spreading the message of animal care by making and sending a postcard?

☐ **Reach out to your Network, older Girl Scouts, and community resources.**

- Community-theater troupes, high-school drama classes or clubs, college dance departments, photo clubs, and classes can all provide help.

- You may be able to find enthusiastic students or Girl Scout Seniors and Ambassadors to provide guidance on making simple costumes or props if you need them, or to offer other assistance.

☐ **Give the girls time to practice, and hold a "dress rehearsal" before the presentation.** There's no need for a "perfect" performance, but practice will allow the girls to feel confident about the message they will deliver.

INSPIRED BY ANIMALS

SAMPLE SESSION 7
Inspired by Animals

AT A GLANCE

Goal: Girls continue to explore how caring for animals resembles caring for themselves and begin to experience the good feelings that caring gives them.

LIMITED TIME? COMBINE SESSIONS 7 AND 8!

If you and the Daisies prefer to spend just one session planning and practicing for the Red Robin Project, simply combine Sessions 7 and 8. Choose which Opening and Closing Ceremonies and snack you prefer, focus in on the "Animal Advertisers" activity, and use the Story Time's "Japanese Garden Yoga" postures to get the girls moving!

- Opening Ceremony: Animals Around the World (Crane: Japan)

- Origami: Turning Paper into Art

- Story Time: "Gloria's Story"

- Animal Riddle Poem

- Snack Time: Fruits from Japan

- Preparing the Red Robin Project

- Closing Ceremony: Sharing Our Knowledge

MATERIALS

- **As Girls Arrive:** paper, crayons, markers

- **Opening Ceremony:** pictures of a crane, opposite page; construction paper, markers, crayons, glue, and assorted craft materials; Team Animal Mural

- **Origami:** origami paper or pieces of colored paper cut into squares (see page 53 in the girls' book for directions)

- **Story Time:** CD player and music

- **Animal Riddle Poem:** large sheet of paper or poster board, marker

- **Snack Time:** see details on page 85

- **Preparing the Red Robin Project:** art and craft materials, or other props or materials the girls may decide on; video camera (if this is what you'll be doing)

PREPARE AHEAD

Talk with any assistants about what they'll do before and during the session.

Prepare and set out the session's snack.

AS GIRLS ARRIVE

Invite the girls to think about a way they enjoy getting exercise, and to draw or describe in words what it is and add it to their All About Me Nests.

 ## Opening Ceremony:
Animals Around the World (Crane: Japan)

Gather the girls in a Daisy Circle and let them know that during Story Time today, Gloria, the morning glory, will share stories about her visit to Japan and tell about some Japanese traditions, which include making animal figures out of paper. Share with the girls that in Japan, a very special kind of bird is the crane. Show them the two crane pictures on this page, explaining that one of them is origami. Then say:

An ancient Japanese legend says if a person folds a thousand origami cranes, then a crane will grant that person a wish, such as living a very long life.

Then share some of these fun facts about Japanese cranes:

- *Japanese cranes (called* tancho *in Japanese) are among the largest of all cranes.*

- *They are 5 feet tall and weigh about 26 pounds. That means they are taller than you!*

- *In Japan, cranes symbolize peace, long life, and good fortune.*

- *Cranes are not the national bird of Japan. Japanese pheasants are! (If you have one available, show the girls a picture of a Japanese pheasant.)*

Paste a picture of a crane on the Team Animal Mural and invite the girls to contribute by adding drawings of the crane's habitat, such as a river, pond, wetlands, shoreline, etc.

Origami: Turning Paper into Art

Now might be a good time to point the girls to pages 52–53 in their book, and pass out pieces of origami or other square-shaped paper. As you guide the girls in making a fun origami shape, you might want to tell them about Florence Temko, an origami expert who taught origami to the world—and to Girl Scouts the world over, too!

Story Time: "Gloria's Story"

Today the girls will hear how Gloria tells her story through movement. When you've read as much as there is time for, invite the girls to look at the "Japanese Garden Yoga" postures shown in their book (pages 50-51). If you've brought music, put it on now to set the mood. Then introduce (and demonstrate!) each of the moves, reminding the girls to start each one with a deep breath in, and finish with a deep breath out:

Pages 40–41 of the girls' book

BIRD IN FLIGHT

Remind the girls about the bird sculpture by Constantin Brancusi on page 49 of their book. When they look at it, can they feel a bird in flight?

The Butterfly: Sitting down, press the bottoms, or soles, of your feet together. Keep your back nice and straight. Now gently rock your knees up and down.

The Turtle: Curl up on the floor. Tuck your knees under your tummy. Round your back as if you were a turtle in a shell. Slowly stretch one arm forward, then slowly bring it back into your "shell." Repeat with one arm at a time, then one leg at a time. Try to stretch your neck, too.

The Crane: Stand on both feet. Lift one leg, and touch your foot to the inside of your other leg, right above or below the knee. Balance. Now try the other side. If you can, bring both arms over your head. Press your palms together.

When the girls have finished their mini-yoga session, ask them how they feel. Let them know that the poses are something that other people might enjoy learning, and that they can teach others to do them—even the audience for their Red Robin Project.

Animal Riddle Poem

As a whole group, have the girls create a short riddle poem describing an animal, but without saying the animal's name. Organize it like this:

- **Line 1:** Describe how the animal looks.

- **Line 2:** Describe or write out the sound the animal makes.

- **Line 3:** Describe the animal's actions.

- **Line 4:** End with: "Who am I?"

Give an example, such as:

> *Soft and furry,*
> *Meow meow all day long*
> *Loves to play with yarn*
> *Who am I?*

Let the girls agree among themselves on what animal to choose. Working together, they can come up with the lines of the poem, which you can record on a large sheet of paper.

EXTRA CHALLENGE!

Invite each girl to create her own Animal Riddle Poem and then challenge the others to guess the mystery animal she's describing.

ICEBREAKER!

The Animal Riddle Poems the girls create can be a great icebreaker activity at their presentation of the Red Robin Project. Ask if one or more of the girls wants to volunteer to recite her poem, and ask the audience to guess what animal it describes.

Snack Time!

Fruits from Japan

As you present the day's snack, explain to the girls that enjoying seasonal fruits is one way people in many countries, including Japan, mark the seasons. Explain that a "seasonal fruit" is a fruit that is picked or harvested at a specific time of the year.

Then invite the girls to enjoy the seasonal fruit from Japan that you've chosen for today, whether strawberries and melons (spring), cherries, peaches, and watermelons (summer), persimmons and Japanese or sand pears (fall), or mandarin oranges (winter).

Whatever form the girls'
Red Robin Project takes,
they will benefit from a few
public-speaking pointers.
*Remember, speaking up
takes confidence and then
boosts it even higher!* So
share these tips:

- *Make sure you have
  everyone's attention before
  you begin speaking. You
  might want to use the
  Girl Scout Quiet Sign and
  teach it to your audience!*

- *Speak loudly but don't
  shout.*

- *Speak clearly.*

- *Speak slowly enough
  so that everyone can
  understand you.*

 ## Preparing the Red Robin Project

Use this time to let the girls prepare the project:

- The girls can decide what they'd like to talk about at the booths or exhibits or in front of the mural.

- They can make any needed props, such as puppets, posters, animal images, bookmarks, a handout, and invitations or other items to advertise their project.

- They can run through the "Busy Squirrels Song and Dance," a "Japanese Garden Yoga" demonstration, or whatever they choose.

- If possible, you can even videotape some activities to show to an audience.

- Or the girls may choose drawings or other items from their All About Me Nests and put them together to create a booklet to share with the audience that shows how caring for animals is like caring for themselves.

Closing Ceremony: Sharing Our Knowledge

Ask girls to come together again in a Daisy Circle so they can each name something they've learned about animals from a family member, friend, teacher, or someone or something else—even a story! After everyone has shared, let the girls know that sharing what we know is important. Say something like:

- *When we know something, it's nice to share it with others.*

- *At a future gathering, you will earn your Red Robin Award by sharing what you know about caring for animals with others, so that they will care for animals, too.*

- *You'll see how good it feels to share what you know with others!*

Looking Ahead to Session 8

- At their next gathering, the girls will learn how advertisers use attractive packaging to get people to buy their products. To do so, they'll taste test three different brands of the same flavor yogurt: one that uses cute animals on its packaging, and two that don't. Tap your Network to gather yogurts and other needed materials, such as bowls and plastic spoons.

- The yogurt can also serve as the snack for the gathering, or you might prepare a panda-inspired snack of black-and-white foods, such as black bean dip and jicama sticks.

- Reach out to your Network for poster board, bookmark-size cardboard, colored paper or invitation blanks, colored markers, and any other needed art supplies for any props or creative items the Daisies will make for their Red Robin Project.

- If you have time to "go all out" with the Red Robin Project, check in with Network volunteers who are providing technical and other assistance as the Daisies continue to prepare and practice.

Learning how and why ads use animals—that makes Daisies confident consumers!

WHAT ANIMALS TELL US

SAMPLE SESSION 8
What Animals Tell Us

AT A GLANCE

Goal: Girls strengthen their communication skills as they progress on their Red Robin Project.

- Opening Ceremony: Animals Around the World (Panda: Japan/China)

- Story Time: "Gloria's Story" (continued)

- Snack Time: Jicama Sticks and Black Bean Dip

- Animal Advertisers

- Creating the Red Robin Project: Using the Power of Animal Advertisers

- Practicing the Red Robin Project

- Closing Ceremony: My Favorite Animal

MATERIALS

- **Opening Ceremony:** picture of panda (page 89); crayons and markers; Team Animal Mural

- **Snack Time:** see page 90

- **Animal Advertisers:** three brands of the same flavor yogurts; two containers of each yogurt brand (one that will be concealed and one displayed); a box or dark paper to conceal containers; plastic spoons

(three for each girl), and three identical bowls or cups in the same color

- **Creating the Red Robin Project:** poster board, bookmark-size cardboard, colored paper or invitation blanks, and colored markers; various art supplies as needed (depending on the girls' project)

PREPARE AHEAD

Set up the blind taste test of the yogurt. Pour the yogurt from the three containers into three bowls without any girls watching. (Be sure you know which bowls hold which brands.) Display the three containers (but not in front of the bowl they represent). Conceal the empty containers in some way, such as putting a box over them or covering the labels with dark paper. Place each concealed container next to the bowl that contains that yogurt. Have a second set of the same containers out in the open for the girls to see which products they will taste.

Prepare and set out the snack if you are serving something other than the yogurt.

 ## Opening Ceremony: Animals Around the World (Panda: Japan/China)

Gather the girls in a Daisy Circle and ask them to take turns sharing one thing about animals and animal care that they've learned along this journey. Let them know that they will hear more about Gloria's trip to Japan during Story Time today, and that during her trip she sees a Giant Panda.

Then share some of these fun facts about the Giant Panda:

- *Giant Pandas are known and loved all around the world, but pandas are very rare. There are only about 1,000 of them still living in the wild. They are an "endangered species." That means if special care isn't taken, they might disappear altogether.*

- *Giant Pandas aren't giant when they are born. Newborn pandas are about the size of a stick of butter. But they grow to be about 5 or 6 feet tall and weigh about 275 pounds.*

- *Giant Pandas eat bamboo. They eat about 80 pounds of it every day. They spend about 16 hours a day eating! That's more than half a day!*

Invite girls to say a word or phrase to describe the panda (cute, cuddly, big, eats a lot, etc.) and add it to their Team Animal Mural on their own or with your help. They can also say a word or phrase about how they feel when they think about the panda, and add that, too.

The panda in "Gloria's Story," girls' book, page 45

Story Time: "Gloria's Story" (continued)

During Gloria's trip to Japan, she learns that the Giant Panda is a gift from the people of China to the people of Japan. Before you continue "Gloria's Story," ask the girls to notice how Gloria pretends to be a panda. After they hear the story, ask them to take turns pretending to be their favorite animal.

Animal Advertisers

Start by letting the girls know they are about to participate in a blind taste test to learn about how packaging might make them want or not want certain things. Explain that a blind taste test is a way to taste things without knowing exactly what they are, so that you decide how much you like them based only on their taste. Point out that companies often use blind taste tests to compare their product to other companies' products. You might say:

To be fair, the tasters do not know, or are "blind to," which products are which as they taste them. Do any of you recall which flower friend represents being fair? (Answer: Lupe, the Lupine. The girls might know of Lupe from the poster of the flower friends and their values of the Girl Scout Law, or from taking another Girl Scout leadership journey.)

Then say something like: *Today you will taste three kinds of yogurt without knowing which brand is which. One of the brands uses an animal on its containers and its labels.*

Before they taste, ask the girls to look at the containers that are not concealed and say which brand they think will taste best, and why. Record their answers for comparison after the taste test.

Invite the girls to taste each yogurt using a new, or freshly washed, spoon with each taste. As they taste, ask which they like better and why. When all the girls have tasted and chosen their favorite, unveil the concealed yogurt containers with a flourish—ta-dah!—and have them compare their choices with the containers.

Discuss the taste test results with the girls, using the following questions to get them talking:

● *Why do you think companies design their packaging with animals?*

● *Which package do you like the best? Why?*

Snack Time!

Jicama Sticks and Black Bean Dip

Now might be a good time to serve a panda-inspired snack of black-and-white foods like black bean dip and jicama sticks. Or you might decide to move directly to the "Animal Advertisers" activity, which centers around a yogurt taste test.

- *What other food or products (e.g., towels, dishes, hats, etc.) do you know of that have animals on their packages or in their commercials?*

- *What matters more to you about what you eat: What the package looks like or what the food tastes like? Why?*

Creating the Red Robin Project: Using the Power of Animal Advertisers

Let the girls know that advertisers use animals in their ads because many people, including children, find animals cute and appealing. Suggest that's something to keep in mind as they prepare their Red Robin Project. Then invite them to make posters, bookmarks, a simple handout, invitations, a mural they can cut up and share, or some other means to advertise their project or get an idea across about animal caring. You might say: *How can we use animal cutouts to attract people to our project?*

Practicing the Red Robin Project

Explain to the Daisies that they'll present their Red Robin Project during the next gathering to the audience they've chosen together. Do a quick run-through to make sure each Daisy knows what she will say and do, starting with the girl or girls presenting the "Animal Riddle Poem" icebreaker, and the girl announcer. Assist the girls with their lines from the script starters on page 81.

After they rehearse, be sure to ask if they have any questions about the project or what they will do.

Closing Ceremony: My Favorite Animal

Gather the girls in a circle and ask them to take turns naming a favorite animal and why they like it. When they've all had a turn, invite them to finish with a friendship squeeze. Remind them that at their next gathering, they will share their knowledge about animal care with an audience. Let them know that you're looking forward to their next Daisy time together.

Looking Ahead to Session 9

The Daisies present their Red Robin Project during the next session, so check in with your Network volunteers for any last-minute assistance, including rounding up postcard materials, if needed: recycled poster board, card stock or recycled folders or boxes, colored markers, pens, pencils—enough for each audience member to make one postcard.

SAMPLE SESSION 9
Teaching Others with Confidence!

AT A GLANCE

Goal: Girls educate and inspire others on animal care, building their own confidence along the way.

- Opening Ceremony
- Presenting the Red Robin Project
- Closing Ceremony: Earning the Red Robin Award

MAKING A DIFFERENCE BOOSTS CONFIDENCE

In this session, the Daisies share ways to care for animals and then invite others to join in the caring. They're being leaders who educate and inspire with confidence!

MATERIALS

- **As Girls Arrive:** All About Me Nests (one for each girl); CD player and music

- **Presenting the Red Robin Project:** any materials and equipment the girls need to present to their

audience, including materials for the postcard-making station (if that's what the girls will do)

- **Closing Ceremony:** Red Robin Awards (one for each girl)

PREPARE AHEAD

- Talk with any assistants about what they'll do before and during the session.

- If the girls are presenting their Red Robin Project via stations or booths, set them up.

- If the girls are presenting a booklet or another item, have it ready to hand out.

- Also set up one (or more) postcard-making stations stocked with postcard blanks, colored markers, pens, pencils, etc., if the girls are asking their audience to pass along their animal care message via postcards.

AS GIRLS ARRIVE

- If possible, invite the girls to display their All About Me Nests so the audience can view them after their Red Robin Project presentation.

If the girls are feeling any pre-presentation jitters or just want to warm up, turn on some music and invite the girls to jump, creep, crawl, fly, leap, and climb like the animals Mari saw in Africa. When the music stops, the girls freeze in place. They can go a few rounds until their guests arrive.

Opening Ceremony

Gather the girls in a circle and ask them each to say one word to describe how they feel as they are about to present their Red Robin Project. If any girls mention feeling excited or nervous, reassure the group that it's OK to feel either way. Let them know it takes courage and strength to speak up about how to care for animals, and that's what they're doing today!

Presenting the Red Robin Project

Have the Daisies greet their guests as they arrive. Once they are settled in their seats, have the girl(s) presenting the icebreaker "Animal Riddle Poem" perform their parts. After the audience has guessed the animal riddle, invite the announcer to introduce the Project as you've prepared:

- *Today our Daisy group will share with you important ways to care for animals and invite you to keep animals safe and sound, and teach others how to do that, too!*

Invite the girls to take their places at their stations or in front of their mural, book, or other art project, or to go "onstage" to perform. When the girls have completed their presentations, let them conclude by asking the audience to pledge to care for animals. Have them say the lines they've practiced, or you might use a few sentences like these:

- *Will you join us in promising to do your best to keep animals safe and sound? If you do, will you keep spreading the message of animal care by making and sending a postcard?*

Then invite the girls to point the audience to the postcard-making station (if that's what they've decided to do), where the guests can view the postcards the girls made and make their own postcards, too, inspired by what they've just learned from the Daisies about caring for animals.

Earning the Red Robin Award

Bring the girls together in a Daisy Circle with their guests around them. Ask the girls to say one word that describes how they feel, now that they've spoken up for animals. Say something like:

- *You did a great job today. You showed courage and strength in speaking up for animals. That makes you all leaders.*

- *And you made the world a better place by teaching and inspiring others. That makes you all leaders, too!*

- *For flying out into the community and sharing your knowledge, you have earned the Red Robin Award.*

Then present each girl with a Red Robin Award.

Looking Ahead to Session 10

Write the names of all the animals the girls have met along the journey on small slips of paper to be used for the "Animal Masks" activity.

Thinking Ahead to Steps for the Tula Award

At the next session, Daisies will move ahead with steps toward the Tula Award, which they will earn at their Final Celebration. To earn the award, the girls will celebrate what they've learned about animal care and self-care and all the good feelings they've experienced on their journey. To celebrate, the girls might use the masks they make in Session 10 and/or the Team Animal Mural and other journey projects. They can also use the script detailed in Session 10 and in the Final Celebration.

Tap your Network for volunteers to assist with all aspects of the celebration. Depending on their expertise, some Network members might be called on to invite the Daisies' families to attend this special session; others might provide specific assistance for the event, including any media needs and snack preparation. Animal-themed snacks would be great to serve. Maybe someone in your Network even knows how to turn fruits and vegetables into cute animal or flower "sculptures" for the snack table! Or consider these ideas:

- Repeat some of the healthy "animal-themed" snacks from the journey, such as "Ants on a Log" (Session 1) and "Apple Ladybugs" (Session 4).

- **Wiggly Animals:** To make and serve fruit-flavored gelatin animals, have the girls use animal-shaped cookie cutters to cut out wiggly animals from pre-prepared pans of gelatin dessert.

- **Shape-Up:** Use mini cookie cutters to cut apples, pears, and other fruits and vegetables into animal shapes.

When girls lead, even in a simple elephant parade, they get a huge confidence boost!

MANY SKILLS TO LEARN

Many Skills to Learn

TAKING THE LEAD WITH CONFIDENCE

As the Daisies take the lead in this session's "Elephant Parade" activity, they build self-esteem and gain confidence. Then, in their Closing Ceremony, they have the opportunity to demonstrate confidence by sharing their feelings about caring for animals with others.

AT A GLANCE

Goal: The girls come to understand how caring for themselves, and caring for animals, makes them feel.

- Opening Ceremony: Animals Around the World (Elephant: Kenya, South Africa, Thailand, India)

- Story Time: "Mari's Story" and Backwards Bingo

- Snack Time: Many-Colored, Wild Parrot Vegetables and Dip

- Elephant Parade

- Animal Masks

- Preparing for the Tula Award and Celebration

- Closing Ceremony: Caring for Animals Makes Me Feel . . .

- Looking Ahead to the Final Celebration

MATERIALS

- **As Girls Arrive:** paper, crayons, markers, craft materials; All About Me Nests (one for each girl)

- **Opening Ceremony:** picture of an elephant, construction paper, markers, crayons, glue, and assorted craft materials; Team Animal Mural

- **Story Time:** bingo cards (one for each girl) photocopied from page 99, and five buttons or other markers per girl; Team Animal Mural

- **Snack Time:** see page 98

- **Elephant Parade:** a simple obstacle maze

- **Animal Masks:** slips of paper, each with the name of an animal on it (two for each girl), and a small container for holding them; paper plates, craft sticks, glue, and other assorted craft materials

- **Preparing for the Tula Award:** slips of paper, each with the name of a Daisy on it, and a hat, bag or small container

PREPARE AHEAD

- Talk with any assistants about what they'll do before and during the session.

- For the bingo game, have the cards and pieces ready (use the sample board on page 99)

- For the "Animal Mask" activity, glue a craft stick to a paper plate, one for each girl.

- For the "Elephant Parade," set up a simple and safe maze for the girls to walk through.

AS GIRLS ARRIVE

Welcome the girls as they arrive, and invite each one to continue filling her All About Me Nest, this time adding an object, picture, and/or words that describe something an adult who takes care of her used to do for her, but that she can now do for herself.

Opening Ceremony: Animals Around the World (Elephant: Kenya, South Africa, Thailand, India)

Gather the girls in a Daisy Circle and ask each one to share what she has added to her All About Me Nest.

Then let the girls know that in today's Story Time, they'll hear how Mari tells about her trip to Africa, including how she saw mother elephants taking care of their babies. Explain that the elephant is the national animal of Kenya, South Africa, Thailand, and India.

Then show the girls the picture of an elephant and share some of these facts:

- *An elephant can eat 300 pounds of food in one day!*

- *An adult elephant's trunk is about 7 feet long. That's as long as some of the world's tallest basketball players!*

- *Elephants have ivory tusks that grow during their whole lives.*

Now invite the girls to add an elephant to their Team Animal Mural.

BABY ELEPHANT

If you have access to the Internet, you might show the girls a video clip of a baby African elephant playing, and listen to the sounds elephants make at http://kids. nationalgeographic.com/ Animals/CreatureFeature/ African-elephant.

**The girls' book,
pages 54–55**

Story Time: "Mari's Story" and Backwards Bingo

Today the Daisies will enjoy "Mari's Story," in which Mari, the marigold, tells the flower friends about seeing some of the largest animals in the world during her visit to Africa.

- Ask the Daisies to listen closely to the story for the sound the baby elephant makes.

- After the reading, invite the girls to play a game of Backwards Bingo, based on Mari's trip. Hand out the bingo cards, and invite a girl to pick and call out the names of the animals! Be sure to monitor your time, as the girls may want to keep on playing!

- Then invite the girls to add some of their bingo cards to their Team Animal Mural. As they do, ask them as a group to imitate the sound the baby elephants made in the story! You might also invite the girls to imitate the sound a parrot might make when it mimics (or "parrots") a lion's roar.

Snack Time!

Many-Colored, Wild Parrot Vegetables and Dip

For a many-colored, healthful snack, serve red, yellow, and green bell-pepper slices, baby carrots or carrot sticks, and broccoli and cauliflower florets with a dip made of 2 parts Greek-style yogurt to 1 part ranch dressing.

BACKWARDS BINGO!

Directions for Backwards Bingo: Each girl gets a copy of this Bingo card and five markers (use buttons or coins) that she can place on any of the squares. When the caller calls out the name of one of her animals, she removes the marker. The girl (or girls) who removes all her markers first is the winner.

TAKE IT OUTDOORS

If the weather is mild, take the parade outdoors to a safe, open space. Each girl can lead her team around benches and branches or over puddles and piles of leaves.

Elephant Parade

Show the girls how to link arms just like elephants link tails. Explain that in this game of trust, each girl will take turns leading the rest of the Daisies through the simple maze of obstacles that you've set up. Guide the girls to give directions, such as "walk five steps to your left" or "take one step forward" to help lead the other Daisies safely through the maze. Let them know this is a great chance for them to show what they can do when they team up! Say something like:

In her story, Mari describes how elephants talk to one another by making rumbling sounds. In this game of trust, your sister Daisies are depending on your ability to communicate clearly and simply to get them through the maze. They're trusting you!

After every girl has had a chance to lead a round of movement, discuss the experience. Ask questions such as these:

- *What was it like to lead and be responsible for getting the girls through the maze?*
- *How did it feel to have to trust one of your sister Daisies so completely?*
- *Were you able to trust the leaders? Why or why not?*
- *Why is trust important?*
- *How did it feel to be a team member getting through the maze successfully based on the directions of your leader?*

Then explain to the Daisies that they will celebrate the end of their journey the next time they meet. Remind them that to earn their Tula Award, they will each tell their story of how they felt when they taught others about caring for animals with their Red Robin Project.

Suggest that the "Elephant Parade" they just had fun with will be a nice addition to their celebration. They can lead their family members and other guests through a maze just like they've led their sister Daisies! If the girls like the idea, ask for a volunteer who will be the celebration's first maze leader.

GET CREATIVE!

Animal Masks

Remind the girls of the many animals Mari saw in Africa, from the wrinkly elephants to the brightly colored parrots. Draw the girls' attention to the mural and point out that all the animals they've been learning about vary in size, shape, color, movement, and more.

- Tell the girls you have written the names of many of the animals they've been learning about on slips of paper.

- Ask each girl to pick two slips from the container.

- Then ask each girl to read the name of her two animals and say one or more ways they are different. If a girl has trouble reading, some good readers in the group may want to help her out. Or you might work with her to sound out the name. Or, better yet, have some Daisies assist from the sidelines, too, as the girls receive their slips of paper.

- To add an extra challenge, you might ask the girls to say one way the animals they've picked are the same and one way they are different. You might start them off by saying something like:

I picked elephant and leopard. One way they are different is that elephants are wrinkly and gray, while leopards are smooth and spotted. One way they are alike is that they both walk on four legs.

- When everyone has had a chance to compare their animals, make the point that just as animals are different, people are also different from one another.

- Give each girl a paper plate with a craft stick. Have each girl choose one of the two animals she picked and not reveal her choice. Now have the girls make masks representing the animal they selected. (If they don't like either animal, they can choose a new animal.) Then have them use the art materials on hand to make their animal masks.

- When all the masks are made, and as time allows, invite each girl to perform in front of the group using her mask. She can make noise, move, and generally act like the animal, challenging the rest of the girls to guess what kind of animal she is.

MATERIALS

- slips of paper, each with the name of an animal on it (two for each girl)

- a small container for holding them

- paper plates, craft sticks, glue, and other assorted craft materials

MULTIPURPOSE MASKS

If the Daisies are having fun with their masks, they can make use of them again during their journey celebration. Each girl can "perform" her animal using her mask, sounds, and movements, and the guests can guess what kind of animal she is.

101

Preparing for the Tula Award and Celebration

Invite the girls to volunteer to take a lead role in the presentations at their upcoming journey celebration. If more than three girls volunteer, put their names in a hat and choose three. Assign each girl one of the following parts to practice today, and at home, before they meet next:

Daisy 1: *As Daisies, we have learned how to care for animals large and small.*

Daisy 2: *By teaching others how to care for animals, too, we've seen how we can create a good change. And that made us feel good about ourselves and our skills.*

Daisy 3: *Now we will share with you the many ways we can all care for animals in our world.*

Allow time for the girls to practice once or twice in this session, as the rest of the Daisies listen and offer their advice.

Closing Ceremony: Caring for Animals Makes Me Feel . . .

Gather the girls in a Daisy Circle and remind them that at their next gathering, which will be their big journey celebration, they will share with their families how educating and inspiring others to care for animals has made them feel.

Let them know that they will also make a promise to continue caring for animals and to keep their Team Birdbath of creativity flowing. Remind them that these are the steps toward earning their Tula Award. Then say something like:

So let's do some practicing of what we're going to say. Let's go around the circle and each finish this sentence:

Caring for animals makes me feel _____.

After all the girls have had a turn, end with a friendship squeeze.

Looking Ahead to the Final Celebration

Continue to reach out to your Network for assistance with any aspects of the journey celebration that still require attention. Finalize any decisions about snacks to serve and music to play. Remind the girls who will introduce the presentations to practice their lines as much as they can before the big day.

If you will have access to the Internet, find some links to pictures, sounds, or video clips of various animals at http://kids.nationalgeographic.com/Animals/ that you can show at the celebration. Or bring some music to play.

Celebrating all they've learned is a true confidence-builder for the Daisies!

THE FINAL CELEBRATION
Celebrate Our Learning!

AT A GLANCE

CELEBRATIONS BUILD CONFIDENCE!

This final journey celebration is a chance for the Daisies to enjoy all their learning, and share it with family and friends. What a great way to reinforce all the confidence they've gained along this journey!

Goal: Daisies celebrate what they've learned and their growing confidence in caring for animals and themselves.

- Opening Ceremony: Animals Around the World

- Animal Riddle Icebreaker

- Story Time: "Back in the Garden"

- Presenting the Tula Award

- Celebration Snacks

- Closing Ceremony: The Journey's End

- Now, It's Time for You to Celebrate!

MATERIALS

- **As Girls Arrive:** paper, crayons, markers, glue, and assorted craft materials; All About Me Nests (one for each girl)

- **Opening Ceremony:** the Girl Scout Promise printed on a large sheet of paper; a camera if you'll be taking photographs

- **Animal Riddle Icebreaker:** slips of paper, each with the name of an animal the girls have met along the journey, and a small bag or container to hold the slips; Team Animal Mural and markers or crayons

- **Presenting the Tula Award:** (for the "Elephant Parade") a simple obstacle maze; any props the girls have decided to use; Team Animal Mural to use as a backdrop, Tula Awards (one for each girl)

- **Celebration Snacks:** fruit and/or vegetables cut into animal shapes; gelatin in a variety of flavors cut into animal shapes. For "Ants on a Log" and "Apple Ladybugs," see Sessions 1 and 4 for ingredients and instructions.

- **Closing Ceremony:** Girl Scout Law printed on a large sheet of paper

PREPARE AHEAD

- Have assistants prepare the snacks for the celebration.

- Write the Girl Scout Promise and Law on large sheets of paper and post them where the guests can see them during the Opening and Closing Ceremonies.

- Think back on everything the Daisies have accomplished during this journey, in terms of caring for animals and gaining confidence in themselves. Be prepared to remind them of their many achievements.

- Set up the room where the girls will perform with seats for guests and space for the girls to present. Have a simple maze set up so that Daisies can lead guests on an "Elephant Parade."

- Display the Team Animal Mural as a backdrop for their performance. Have the Animal Masks and other art the girls made during the journey available to use as needed, including their Team Birdbath and their All About Me Nests.

- If you are using music, have a CD player and CDs on hand.

 ## Opening Ceremony: Animals Around the World

Have the girls form an inner circle and ask their guests to form a circle around them. (Perhaps a Daisy can give these instructions and teach the guests the Girl Scout Quiet Sign, too!)

Ask the girls to say the Girl Scout Promise. Then ask them to repeat it, and invite the guests in the outer circle to say it, too, reading it on the large sheet of paper.

Then ask everyone to join in and imagine how they would feel if they got to see all the animals they've learned about throughout the journey. If you and/ or guests have cameras, take photos of the girls and their expressions of glee, delight, and excitement.

Animal Riddle Icebreaker

While the guests are still in a circle, explain that during this journey, the girls have been learning facts about animals from around the world. Let them know that today the girls will invite their guests to share what they know about animals.

Bring out the bowl or bag filled with the slips of paper with the names of all the animals. Ask a girl to volunteer to pass the bowl or bag around for each guest to choose a slip of paper.

Then invite each guest to read out the animal's name and either imitate it in some way, such as its sound or movement, or offer up one fact about it. If a guest is stumped, let the girls jump in and assist by performing something about the animal or by offering a fact about it.

If the girls are game, now's the time for them to invite their guest to join them by drawing or writing the name of the animals on the Team Animal Mural.

Story Time: "Back in the Garden"

Girls' book, pages 64–65

Invite a guest or two to read the final section of the girls' book, "Back in the Garden." In this section, the flower friends assist Robin, the red robin, in building her nest in preparation for her baby birds. The flower friends have proven to be considerate and caring toward animals both in their garden and far from home. They've shown courage and strength in their quest to care for animals, and learned new skills of which they are very proud.

Encourage the Daisies to discuss the story by asking questions such as:

- In what way are you and your sister Daisies like the flower friends? How have you cared for animals? How have you been courageous?

- *If you could go with any of the flower friends to her homeland and meet the animals there, which place would you go and why?*

- *The flower friends showed their creativity in telling their stories. How have you showed your creativity along the journey? What craft or art project did you like the most?*

You might also ask the family members a few questions, such as:

- *What have you seen your Daisy learn or do along the journey that makes you proud?*

- *What has she told you about animals or about the journey that has surprised you?*

Presenting the Tula Award

Now, ask the guests to line up near the maze. Invite the Daisy playing the lead "elephant" to direct her sister Daisies and their guests through the maze. Once they're through, have the girls invite the guests to sit down or gather around the Team Animal Mural. Quickly hand out any needed props and gather the Daisies in front of the mural. When all is quiet, invite the three narrators to introduce the presentations, as follows:

Daisy 1: *As Daisies, we have learned how to care for animals large and small.*

Daisy 2: *By teaching others how to care for animals, too, we've seen how we can create a good change. And that made us feel good about ourselves and our skills.*

Daisy 3: *Now we will share with you the many ways we can all care for animals in our world.*

After the introduction, have each Daisy step forward to give her animal performance and ask, "Can you guess who I am?" Once the audience has guessed, the Daisy will say how caring for animals makes her feel. After each girl has presented, gather the Daisies and guests together in a Daisy Circle, and together make a promise to care for animals big and small. In a pledge to keep their creativity flowing, have them make the sound of an animal that they like best. Invite the guests to join in.

Finally, present the Tula Award to each girl in honor of her courage and strength for taking on the task of caring for animals, sharing her knowledge with others, and pledging to keep her Birdbath of creativity flowing.

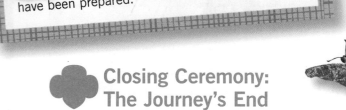

Celebration Snacks

Now's the time to serve and enjoy any animal-themed snacks that have been prepared.

Closing Ceremony: The Journey's End

To conclude this special celebration, and the journey, ask the Daisies to come together once more in a Friendship Circle. As with the Opening Ceremony, invite guests to form an outer circle around the Daisies.

- Display the Girl Scout Law on a large sheet of paper, and have the girls read it aloud.

- Invite the girls to share with their guests how all along this journey they've lived the values of the Girl Scout Law, by making a statement such as, "I cared for animals. I made the world a better place," or, "I spoke up for animals. I am courageous and strong."

- Invite them to go around the circle once more and name one thing they've learned about caring for themselves along the journey. If they need encouragement, you can remind them of their accomplishments.

- Go around one final time, ending with a friendship squeeze.

If the Daisies are continuing in Girl Scouting, use the last few minutes of today's gathering to discuss their upcoming adventures.

Now, It's Time for You to Celebrate!

Congratulations! You've made it to the end of a wonderful journey. Take some time to reflect on your success and your own thoughts about the three keys of Girl Scout leadership.

On this journey of caring for animals, I discovered that I ....

....

....

....

As I guided Daisies to a deeper understanding of caring for animals and

caring for themselves, I connected with ....

....

....

....

After seeing the Daisies' success and enthusiasm, I'm now ready to

Take Action by ....

....

....

....

Every experience in this Daisy *3 Cheers for Animals!* journey is designed to help girls be confident leaders in their daily lives—and in the world!

Discover ➕ **Connect** ➕ **Take Action** ➖ **Leadership**

DISCOVER

Girls understand themselves and their values and use their knowledge and skills to explore the world.

AT THE DAISY LEVEL, girls . . .	RELATED ACTIVITIES (by Session or girls' book chapter/activity)	
Girls develop a strong sense of self.	are better able to recognize their strengths and abilities.	All All About Me Nests; S1: Building a Team Birdbath; S2: Closing Ceremony; S3: Make Meaning of Music; S4: Birdbath Award; S6: The Power of a Postcard, Comparing the Caring, Closing Ceremony; S7: Closing Ceremony; S8: Closing Ceremony; S9: Red Robin Award; Final Celebration: Tula Award; GB: All Tell Your Story, Welcome to this Amazing Animal Adventure, Mari's Story, Elephants and Me, Back in the Garden
Girls develop positive values.	begin to understand the values inherent in the Girl Scout Promise and Law.	All Story Times; S1: Closing Ceremony; S2: Closing Ceremony; S5: Opening Ceremony; GB: All Chapters
	recognize that their choices of actions or words have an effect on others and the environment.	S3: Choices, Choices; S6: Comparing the Caring; GB: All Chapters
Girls gain practical life skills—girls practice healthy living.	gain greater knowledge of what is healthy for mind and body.	All Snack Times; S2: Animals Safe and Sound, Closing Ceremony; S4: Birdbath Award, Busy Squirrels Song and Dance; S7: Story Time with Japanese Garden Yoga; GB: A Purr-fect Surprise in the Garden, My Energy Snacks, Exercises to Try with Friends, Pandas and Me!, Japanese Garden Yoga, Mari's Story, Healthy Habits
Girls seek challenges in the world.	demonstrate increased interest in learning new skills.	All Animals Around the World Opening Ceremonies, and animal care and art activities; S2: Animals Safe and Sound; S5: Field Trip; S6: The Power of a Postcard, Closing Ceremony; Final Celebration: Animal Riddle Icebreaker; GB: All Words for the Wise, profiles, and fact and activity pages
Girls develop critical thinking.	recognize that the thoughts and feelings of others can vary from their own.	S3: Choices, Choices; S5: Animals Talk and So Do We; S8: Animal Advertisers; GB: Pandas and Me!

S=Session, GB=Girls' Book

CONNECT

Girls care about, inspire, and team with others locally and globally.

	AT THE DAISY LEVEL, girls...	RELATED ACTIVITIES (by Session or girls' book chapter/activity)
Girls develop healthy relationships.	are better able to demonstrate helpful and caring behavior.	All Story Time conversations among Flower Friends; S3: Choices, Choices; Closing Ceremony; S4: Birdbath Award; S6: Comparing the Caring; GB: Back in the Garden
	are better able to identify and communicate their feelings to others.	All Story Time conversations among Flower Friends; S3: Choices, Choices; S5: Sounds of Nature Walk; Animals Talk and So Do We; S6: Comparing the Caring; S9: Opening Ceremony, GB: Tell a Story Without Words, A Bird in Space, Back in the Garden
Girls promote cooperation and team building.	begin to learn how to work well with others.	All Team Animal Murals; S1: Building a Team Birdbath; S2: Team Animal Mural; S3: Spin-a-Tale, Choices, Choices; S5: What Animal Am I?; S10: Elephant Parade; GB: Back in the Garden
Girls advance diversity in a multicultural world.	recognize that it's OK to be different.	S4: Story Time; Fantastical Animal Flip Book; GB: A Little Birdie Told Me, If I Were a Bird, Not All Robins Are Red, Zinni's Story, Gloria's Story
	increasingly relate to others in an inclusive manner.	S4: Story Time

TAKE ACTION

Girls act to make the world a better place.

	AT THE DAISY LEVEL, girls...	RELATED ACTIVITIES (by Session or girls' book chapter/activity)
Girls can identify community needs.	gain increased knowledge of their communities' assets.	S2: Animals Safe and Sound; S6: Comparing the Caring
Girls are resourceful problem solvers.	learn the basics of planning a project.	S3: Choices, Choices; S6: Comparing the Caring; S7: Preparing the Red Robin Project; S8: Creating the Red Robin Project, Practicing the Red Robin Project
Girls advocate for themselves and others.	recognize that they can act on behalf of others.	S3: Choices, Choices; S4: Birdbath Award; S6: The Power of a Postcard, The Power of a Postcard 2; S9: Presenting the Red Robin Project
Girls educate and inspire others to act.	are better able to assist peers and seek help from them.	S6: The Power of a Postcard, The Power of a Postcard 2; Closing Ceremony; S7: Closing Ceremony; S9: Presenting the Red Robin Project
Girls feel empowered to make a difference.	feel their actions and words are important to others.	S1 & S4: Closing Ceremony; S6: The Power of a Postcard 2, Comparing the Caring; S7: Closing Ceremony; S9: Presenting the Red Robin Project, Red Robin Award; S10: Closing Ceremony; GB: all profiles, Welcome to this Amazing Animal Adventure, Back in the Garden

The Flower Friends and Their Girl Scout Law Values